REPORTAGE PRESS

ABOUT THE AUTHORS

Shireen Anabtawi is a former Director of Public Relations at the Palestinian Investment Agency in Ramallah, and currently works for the Palestinian Permanent Mission to the UN in Geneva.

Daniela Norris worked for the Israeli Foreign Service for seven years and later was an adviser to the Permanent Mission of Israel at the UN in Geneva. She is now a freelance journalist and writer.

)

REPORTAGE PRESS

Published by Reportage Press
26 Richmond Way, London W12 8LY, United Kingdom
Tel: 0044 (0)20 8749 2867
Email: info@reportagepress.com
www.reportagepress.com

Published by Reportage Press 2010

British Library Cataloguing in Publication Data.

A catalogue record for this book is available from the British Library.

ISBN: 9781906702212

Cover design by Henrietta Molinaro and Kate Gibb

Layout by Florence Production Ltd

Printed and bound in Great Britain by Cromwell Press Group

CROSSING QALANDIYA

Exchanges Across the
Israeli/Palestinian Divide

BY DANIELA NORRIS AND SHIREEN ANABTAWI

To Daphne,
Warm wishes

Daniela Norris

REPORTAGE PRESS

ENDORSEMENTS

"This limpid writing stops doublespeak and propaganda in their tracks, melting in its honesty and good humour. As the friendship deepens on paper, Daniela and Shireen make one fact touchingly clear for the whole world; Israelis and Palestinians are, as Shireen puts it, 'simply people'." – Martina Evans, novelist and poet

"An in-depth look at the Israeli-Palestinian conflict reveals an amazing phenomenon: the hostility between the two peoples is not as great as reflected in the declarations of the leadership of both sides. The intimate correspondence between the two young mothers, Palestinian Shireen Anabtawi and Israeli Daniela Norris poses a painful question: what is all the pointless bloodshed for? Crossing Qalandiya is a moving human document, and at the same time provides wise guidance to all the other peoples in conflict." – Sami Michael, author and the President of the Association for Civil Rights in Israel

"Most 'peace talks' in conflict situations rarely involve much that is peaceful or that involves genuine communication. If only they could take as their model the relationship between Daniela and Shireen, the authors of the letters in this moving, powerful book. These are true 'peace talks'; they speak honestly, with humanity and respect, discussing what is familiar – children, family – but not refraining from asking – and answering – the most difficult and tragic of questions, the ones that keep the two 'sides' apart. Through their 'peace talks', Shireen and Daniela tear down the veil of 'other', shaming those of us who never tried to peer beyond it. What they leave standing is that which we all share: what it means to be human." – Tania Hershman, author

"Peace, living together and security for all are possible." – Dr. Ibrahim Khraishi Ambassador, Permanent Observer of Palestine to the United Nations, Geneva and member of P.L.O. Central Council

"*Crossing Qalandiya* is a wonderful and hopeful book. For me, it shows clearly why women will, in the next decade or two, be at the forefront of the struggle to change from a culture of war to a culture of peace. And not only in Israel and Palestine, but also everywhere else in the world." – Dr. Zeki Ergas, Writers for Peace Committee of International P.E.N. and Secretary General of PEN Suisse Romand Center

"If you never read another book, read this one! Brilliant. Two women, one Israeli Jewish, the other Palestinian Arab Muslim meet and, to their surprise, become friends. They exchange frank letters revealing the problems and experiences of their daily lives that neither had known and that were caused by the opposing side, 'the enemy'. They gradually learn to see and understand the other's situation and point of view without completely relinquishing their own. If all the politicians would read this book and talk and listen to each other as these two women have, there would be no more Middle East conflict." – Jean Currie, the Society of Women Writers and Journalists

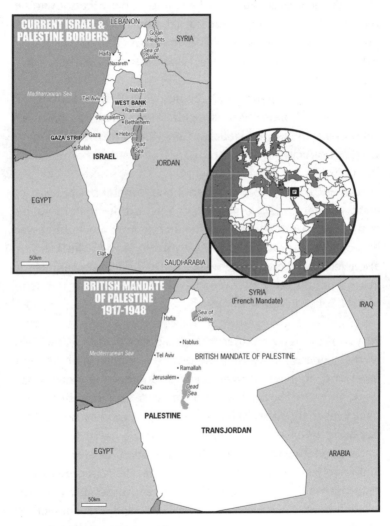

Maps by Lawrence Goldsmith

CROSSING QALANDIYA

Geneva, March 2008. Daniela Norris and Shireen Anabtawi meet for the first time. Shireen is Palestinian, Daniela – Israeli.

"When Daniela invited me for lunch at her house, together with my husband and children, I didn't want to go," confesses Shireen. "Over the last decade, the only Israelis I'd had contact with were soldiers, and in my eyes all the Israelis were the same – occupiers and enemies."

Shireen's husband was the one to convince her to go. And from this visit, a friendship was born; a deep, generous friendship that developed with time. The two met in Geneva many times over several months, with and without other family members. Every encounter opened another window into the other's life, and brought smiles to their lips, and sometimes tears to their eyes.

Shireen and Daniela both knew that when they returned to their homelands, Daniela to Tel Aviv and Shireen to Ramallah, there would be many obstacles and road-blocks in the way of their friendship. An exchange of letters seemed like a natural way to keep it alive.

Daniela speaks Hebrew, Shireen Arabic – two sister, Semitic languages. They don't speak each other's languages. A third language, English, had to connect the two. For many months, they wrote to each other late at night, after their families had gone to bed. Shireen wrote in Arabic, Daniela in Hebrew, and they later translated the letters to English, so they could both fully understand their content.

The two women did not think they could offer solutions to the complicated situation in their region. But they understood that they held a power greater than that of politicians or the military – they are two women, on two opposite sides of the conflict, and they can contribute to the mutual understanding of their peoples in a way no political or military leader can. The more exchanges they had, the more open they became. And

1

the more they believed that without the social and human dimension there can be no real solution and resolution to the conflict.

These letters express a candid wish to share the friendship they have found with others, on both sides of this bloody conflict. Others who have not had the good fortune and opportunity to personally meet "the other", those whom their generation has learned to call "The Enemy".

Shireen (*left*) and Daniela (*right*). Photographed by Ines Garcia Baena.

SOME NAMES AND LOCATIONS HAVE BEEN CHANGED, BUT THE REALITY OF SHIREEN'S AND DANIELA'S LIVES IN PALESTINE AND ISRAEL REMAINS THE SAME.

CROSSING QALANDIYA

April 18th, 2008
Tel Aviv

Dear Shireen,

I hope you are well, and that you remember me. We met in Geneva last month, at a cocktail party at Michelle's house. I admit that I was taken aback when you said you were from Palestine. I was convinced you were Italian or Greek – something Mediterranean, anyway – but I didn't imagine you were Palestinian.

Michelle introduced us and glided away. Now I know why she was smiling. I am sure she was quite pleased with herself when she saw we continued talking to each other for the rest of the evening.

It is strange, but despite the few kilometres that set us apart, I have never really gotten to know a Palestinian woman. Certainly not one as charming as you – pretty, beautifully dressed, speaking fluent English. What can I say? I am embarrassed to admit that the image I had of Palestinians was somewhat different.

But I was taken with your smile and your green eyes, and when we discovered that we had children of similar ages, our curiosity overcame our suspicion and we started speaking openly like friends. I can't recall how long we spoke, but as we noticed that we were among the last to leave, an incredible thing happened – we decided to meet the next morning for a cup of coffee.

I have a confession: I hesitated before I went to meet you the next morning. After all, you are supposed to be "The Enemy", and who knows what The Enemy has in store for them? But we said we'd bring our kids along, and when I arrived with my two little boys and saw you waiting at the café with your two beautiful children, I was ashamed of my previous thoughts.

It was not a long encounter, but the pleasantness of it lingers in my mind. It affected me deeply. By the time we had finished drinking our coffees, the children had overcome the language barrier, as only children can, and had started running around and making too much noise. Then came the time to say goodbye, and we exchanged addresses in Tel Aviv and Ramallah.

You said it was easy for us to talk in Geneva, but would be much more difficult once we were back in our homeland. I hope it isn't so, and that you are glad to receive my letter. Ever since I met you, I read and listen to the news from our region differently, with more compassion for the other side – your side. Every time someone mentions Ramallah I think of you, and wonder how you are, what you're thinking, what you're now feeling towards us, Israelis. And I would like to know more about your daily life. Do you remember our encounter sympathetically, as I do?

Yours,
Daniela

* * *

May 10th, 2008
Ramallah

Dear Daniela,

Your letter reached me only yesterday, three weeks after it was sent. This is hardly surprising, as our postal services do not function very well. I am not mentioning this to complain; I am just worried that you'll think your letter was lost or, even worse, that I don't want to correspond with you.

I appreciate your frankness. I must admit that the only Israelis I've met over the past years have been the soldiers at road-blocks, and I, too, found it strange to meet an Israeli woman with whom I was able to connect so easily. When I was seventeen I did attend meetings of "Peace Now"[1], despite my parents' objections. But nothing came of it.

In those meetings we sat alongside Israeli youths, and discussed the situation. We talked and talked, and we even felt that we could understand each other. But just a few months later they had to go to the army, and we went back to our lives, and despite the hope we all had that things would improve, they only got worse.

You ask about my daily life in Ramallah. I hope that one day you'll be able to visit me here. Ramallah is beautiful. When I was in Europe and said I was from Ramallah, people asked me whether we had roads, shops, food. I was surprised to hear these questions. It's so sad that this is the image we have in the eyes of the world.

---

1 "Peace Now" is the largest extra-parliamentary movement in Israel and the country's oldest peace movement. It was founded in 1978 during the Israeli-Egyptian peace talks. See www.peacenow.org.il.

Ramallah is an amazing city, and has fantastic shops and cafés which are full every evening. I am sure that if you saw it you would hardly believe your eyes. Our main problem in Ramallah is that we feel trapped. It is difficult to travel from one place to the next, and there aren't many places to go, anyway.

I have a dream, not a very significant one, but a dream nonetheless. I dream of driving in fourth gear. It never happens here, as there is nowhere to drive. When we travelled through Europe we hired an automatic car, and my husband joked that it must be our destiny, never to drive in fourth gear.

What else can I tell you? Not long ago we bought a house, and furnished it with antique-style decor. My son, Saif, is two years old, and a few months ago he stopped wearing nappies, so it is much easier now. My mother took him over to her house for three days and, as if by magic, he came back nappy-free.

My mother is an amazing woman. You know, in our society families are very closely knit, not like in Europe. When I was in Europe I met people who lived 400 km from their elderly parents, but only visited them twice a year. I met elderly people living alone, because their children were too far away or too busy to look after them. In our society this would not happen – looking after one's elderly parents is a sacred duty.

So all in all, my life here is pretty good, but I must admit that it is difficult to come back to Ramallah after spending time in Europe. When we travelled, we drove from country to country and were rarely asked to show a passport. Here, if I want to visit my family in Nablus, I have to show documentation and permits; not only that, but I have to wait long hours at road-blocks, in the heat or in the rain.

I apologise. Perhaps it sounds as if I am complaining, but you asked about my life, so I am telling you. I'll tell you one more story, about my wedding day.

On that day there was a curfew in Nablus and Ramallah, and my husband (who is from Ramallah) couldn't come to my parents' house in Nablus to accompany me to the wedding, as is our tradition. I was worried for his safety, and didn't want him to have to travel back and forth from Ramallah to Nablus which, under normal circumstances, only takes forty minutes each way.

So my parents and I decided to make our own way to Ramallah, to the venue of the wedding. But on our way we were stopped by a young soldier – nineteen at most.

"Where are you going?" he asked.

"I am getting married today," I said. "Look, this is my wedding dress."

I showed him my dress, and he looked the other way.

"You can't pass this way," he said. "There's a curfew."

"Please," I begged. "I'm getting married today, and I have to make it to Ramallah. I can go through the hills, but it would be so much easier to travel on the road. I don't want my wedding dress to be ruined."

"Go home," he said. "There's a curfew."

I took out the wedding invitation and showed it to him.

"I don't read Arabic," he said. "Go home."

So we turned back, and in the village of 'Till we found a man with a donkey who was prepared to take us through the hills and only charge ten shekels – so we started on the winding back-roads from Nablus to Ramallah. And I have to tell you, Daniela, it was one of the most amazing experiences of my life.

The moon hung over the hills and the man with the donkey had a small battery-operated radio which he turned on for us. The full moon and the lively music brought back some of the joy that had been taken from me, and as we approached Ramallah and our family members and friends saw me, wearing my wedding dress, they all applauded, and surrounded us with greetings and warmth. It was a wedding from another world.

Now it's your turn to tell me more about your life. I look forward to hearing from you soon.

Yours,
Shireen

★   ★   ★

May 24th, 2008
Tel Aviv

Dear Shireen,

I was delighted to receive your letter and – despite the delay – I had a feeling you would write back. I only actually received your letter this morning, more than a month after I'd written to you, and perhaps it would be easier to switch to emails, but there is something magical about writing letters . . . do you agree?

It is so strange that you live less than one hour's drive away. If I were a little braver, I would just get in the car and drive to meet you, but things are not that simple, are they? To tell the truth, if I were a little braver, I would probably have shown more interest in the past in how "the other side" lives. But you know, things are not that simple here, either.

Since the beginning of the *intifada*, the Palestinian uprising, and all the suicide bombings, there isn't a real will to try and understand "the other side" – your side. And why should we make an effort to understand? Yesterday, for example, I drove from Ramat Gan to Tel Aviv, normally a twenty minute drive. Suddenly, without warning, the highway was closed. There was a suspicious parcel in one of the road-side bus stops. Police cars drove past, sirens roaring, and I had to wait in the car with two restless kids for nearly an hour while they dismantled the suspected-bomb.

Then we went to the shopping mall in Ramat Gan and, as always, there was the nagging feeling that something bad might happen – there have been so many attempted bombings in shopping centres. How can you live like that, and still want to understand the perpetrators of these atrocities? The mindset is so alien, and their actions so inexplicable . . .

I apologise. I, too, don't mean to complain. But it is important that we understand each other. Maybe if we begin to understand, it will be easier to accept the situation and perhaps even start changing it.

It is really amazing for me to realise that you are the first Palestinian woman I have ever gotten to know, and I am thirty-six years old. After all, we are practically neighbours. And there are so many others like me, living a normal life – or what we pretend is a normal life – in central Israel, despite the fact that there is a war going on in the south, on the border with Gaza. I really don't understand why it has to be so complicated.

This will be a short letter, because Ben, who is the same age as your son Saif, won't let me continue. So I will take him for a walk and post this letter. And, to compensate, I am enclosing a photograph of me with my two boys, Ron and Ben.

Yours,
Daniela

★   ★   ★

May 31st, 2008
Ramallah

Dear Daniela,

Thank you for your letter and the photograph you sent. I put it on our fridge so I can look at it every day, and when Saif and Ghazal ask me about it, I can explain to them that these are our Israeli friends.

You know, Saif is afraid of Israelis, because the only Israelis he knows are soldiers. Sometimes, when he is naughty, I tell him that the soldiers will come. It really isn't right that I do this, but I never thought about it before today.

Ghazal will be six in August, and she is a very clever girl. She can't sit quietly even for a moment; she's just like a boy.

She already asks questions which I find hard to answer, but I am doing my best.

Yesterday we went to visit my parents in Nablus, and I remembered that when I was Ghazal's age, we'd always go and visit the coastal city of Natanya. We'd take a stroll by the sea and eat ice cream. Natanya is only twenty minutes away from Nablus, and every time we felt like going there we'd simply get in the car and drive. These days, who could even imagine such a thing?

I asked my father if he remembered this, and he didn't want to talk about it. He said that those were different days.

I am sad that my children don't see anything other than the present situation. Do you know that until about five or six years ago, Nablus was a beautiful place to live? We had nice shops, and pavements, and even a small pond with ducks swimming in it. Now the children don't even have a proper playground to play in.

There was a weekend market, and all the residents of Nablus used to park their cars far from the city centre so as to leave the parking spaces for the visitors, because we knew it was good for commerce. Today, we've got nothing.

The first thing that was destroyed when the tanks rolled into town was the pavements. We had new, modern parking meters, just like in Europe. They are gone, too. And no one wants to invest the money in fixing the pavements and the parking meters, because there is no money for such things. And even if there was, there's a high chance that it would all be destroyed again.

I know that your people went through a tragedy, too. When I see films and programmes about the Holocaust on

11

television, they always make me cry. But I cannot help asking myself, and I hope you won't mind if I ask you too – why do we have to pay the price?

It was the Nazis who did all those horrible things, not us, so why were we the ones who had to give up our homes and our lands so you could have your Israeli State? Why do you, who came from all over the world, have more of a right to this land than we, who were born here?

Maybe I shouldn't have written that last paragraph, but I have, and I will send this letter as it is. And I hope that you can give me some answers that will help me understand – because I really want to.

As you wrote, perhaps if *we* can understand each other, there is a chance for mutual understanding between our peoples, after all.

Yours,
Shireen

★　★　★

June 14th, 2008
Tel Aviv

Dear Shireen,

You have no idea how much I appreciate your frankness, and I intend to be just as candid with you because, otherwise, what's the point?

My grandmother had a number tattooed on her forearm. She was in Auschwitz, but she survived. Her parents, her husband and her siblings were murdered by the Nazis, along with six million others. Six million people, systematically murdered. Can you grasp this number? Even for me, it is hard to comprehend.

She never talked about it – maybe because she didn't want to, or maybe because I was too young and too preoccupied with other things. In any case, when the State of Israel was founded she, and hundreds of thousands of others like her, suddenly had hope. The same old hope that Jews have had for centuries – to return to the Holy Land, the land of their forefathers – Israel.

It is true that the Zionist movement had started at the end of the 19th century, fifty years and more before the Holocaust, but it was only after the Holocaust that most countries recognised the right of the Jews to a state of their own in the land of Israel. Why did you have to pay the price? you ask. Good question.

The only answer I can give you is the answer that I was taught to give: if, in 1948, the Palestinians and our other Arab neighbours had accepted the right of the State of Israel to exist, then we would have had no reason to make your life difficult over the past sixty years.

It is true that the Holocaust was not your fault, and it is true that your grandparents' generation had to give up homes and lands. But *my* grandparents' generation had to go through the Holocaust. Neither of them has chosen this destiny.

The important question is not whose fault is what happened in the past, but what can be done now in order to change the present, and the future, so that your children and my children can play together one day, instead of fighting.

Yours,
Daniela

★   ★   ★

June 19th, 2008
Ramallah

Dear Daniela,

It's unbelievable, your letter made it to Ramallah in three days. Perhaps there is hope after all!

You are right, there is no point in crying over the past, but it is a fact that at least three generations of Palestinian children have been born into and grown up under occupation. I am sure you know that in our eyes you are The Occupying Power, even if you like to pretend that you are not. And how can you deny it? The Israelis are controlling our borders, the check-points, our movement, what we can have and what we cannot. Food, medication, building materials, fuel, weapons – everything.

Even now, when we have a moderate government and there is a window of opportunity which you could use to solve the problem once and for all, you are hesitating. There is always a reason or an excuse not to do things.

Do you know, Daniela, that from the moment our children learn to walk, they also learn to throw stones? Not because this is in our blood, because our blood is not

14

different to yours (despite what some of you think), and not because Palestinian children like to throw stones. It's because the reality they see around them is one of occupation, of a foreign army that controls and limits what we do in our daily lives. So of course they throw stones. What else can they do?

And the longer the occupation lasts, the more and more generations of Palestinian children who will be born into it.

Why do my people deserve to live in destroyed towns and in refugee camps? And why should you, in your beautiful cities by the sea, feel safe, while only half an hour away others live in refugee camps and under occupation?

Well, this is somewhat more than I intended to write, and the disadvantage, or perhaps advantage, of pen and paper is that from the moment the ink has dried, it is difficult to erase. Of course I could start again, but I don't intend to. So I'm afraid that once more you will receive a letter which may not make you happy, but is frank and comes straight from the heart.

I believe that as a mother, you, too, wouldn't want your children to grow up in an atmosphere of oppression and violence.

I already told you how much Saif fears soldiers. Do you know that every time he hears gun shots, he freezes and becomes pale with anxiety? And he is only two years old, so I can still control what he does. But for how long will I be able to control him? When he's ten or eleven, if we're still under occupation, he will want to go with all his friends and throw stones at the soldiers. They don't have playgrounds; they don't have sports centres, so this is what they do every day. Would you want your Ben to grow up like that?

Yours,
Shireen

★   ★   ★

June 24th, 2008
Tel Aviv

Dear Shireen,

I think you are right; the postal service between Tel Aviv and Ramallah is improving. It took your letter only six days to reach me and, when I read it, it made me cry.

As a mother, it makes me sad to think that your adorable children are afraid of soldiers and don't have a playground to play in, when we have a fantastic one just two minutes away. Maybe one day Saif and Ghazal will be able to come and play here, with us.

But as an Israeli, I cannot but think immediately of my children, who are scared of suicide bombers, and the children in southern Israel, who endure daily rocket attacks, and can't even go to school every day like normal children should.

So you may say: if my children can't have a decent life, why should yours? I can understand this position. On the other hand, I cannot understand why you teach your children to hate us, and how exactly we are supposed to achieve peace, when entire generations of Palestinian children learn to hate Jews and Israelis.

Why do your schoolbooks poison your children against us? And if they learn to throw stones as soon as they learn to walk, how can we ever make peace with you?

I told my parents about our correspondence, and how you made such an impression on me in Geneva. My parents are average Israelis, living in a three bedroom flat in a suburb of Tel Aviv.

They are both architects. My step-father is a fifth-generation Israeli born man, and my mother emigrated from Romania nearly forty years ago, when she was twenty-something, together with my father, who is now remarried and living in Canada.

They were all very surprised that such an exchange with a Palestinian is even possible, because they've never had one themselves. Of course, they know and work with Israeli Arabs, but this is a totally different thing – at least in their eyes.

Our history books say that you and they are the same people, but you are those who did not recognise our state when it was founded, while they did and agreed to live with and among us. They took on Israeli citizenship and Israeli ID cards, and this makes them a totally different species in our eyes, despite the fact that I'm sure they don't have an easy time as Arabs in a Jewish state. But still, it must be easier than being Palestinian, at least in daily life.

When I was little, I used to spend a lot of time with my grandparents, because both my parents worked long hours. I really liked to listen to my grandmother's stories, and one of my favourites was a tale about a monster called "Bao Bao". This monster would come and eat naughty little children, and sometimes, when I was particularly unruly, my grandmother used to say, half jokingly: "Be careful, or the Bao Bao will come and get you."

I think we turned out to be the Bao Bao for your children, and you turned out to be the Bao Bao for ours. And I have no idea how this can change in the foreseeable future, if they don't get to know each other other than through television screens and the scopes of rifles.

Yours,
Daniela

★   ★   ★

July 3rd, 2008
Ramallah

Dear Daniela,

I hope my letter finds you and your family in good health. I must admit that I have become completely addicted to our letter exchange.

After a long day of work, looking after the children and, of course, some housework for dessert, I am sitting here quietly and telling you what is going on in my mind.

I don't always know where to start, because there is so much I want to say to you. Perhaps I will start by writing how sorry I am about what happened yesterday in Jerusalem[2]. I don't really know what to say, and it is difficult to express

---

2 On July 2nd, 2008, a Palestinian man ploughed an enormous construction vehicle into cars, buses, and pedestrians on a busy street in Jerusalem, killing three people and wounding at least forty-five before he was shot dead by security officers.

what I feel. On one hand, I feel really bad about what happened to innocent people. On the other hand, I feel very bad about what will happen to the family of the perpetrator. After all, they are innocent people, too.

You know, it is very confusing, because each side thinks that they are right, and there is no one to explain each position to the other. But there's one thing I am certain of – no action comes out of thin air. We have a proverb that says: if you know the reason, you will not be surprised by the result.

I believe that in order to solve the problems, we need to know the reasons things happen. Because no one, especially not a young man who has his life ahead of him, a father of two little children, would give up his life and do something like this without a reason.

We must learn from things that happen, to make sure that they don't happen again. My husband and I have discussed this at length over the past two days, and asked ourselves many questions. We have not found answers to all of them.

Do we agree, in any way, with what has happened? Is this acceptable in our religion, or is it a sin? Do actions like this carry any benefit, to anyone? Our answers were confused, just like our lives.

To the first question, whether it is possible to agree with or to support what happened in any way, our answer was that it is something that simply breaks our hearts – especially as among all the killed and wounded, it is very possible that there were some who support or supported the idea of peace with us, Palestinians.

Some of the wounded were children, and I cannot hide the fact that since I met you and your two wonderful children, I think about things differently. I am simply in love with your little boy.

On the other hand, it is impossible to forget that we are a people who have suffered a lot, and we continue to suffer. There are many reasons in our daily lives for people to simply lose their minds. We are thirsty for peace, we dream of our own state, we dream of being free to move from place to place and to work with dignity. We want our children to be able to live in peace.

The second question we asked ourselves was this: is an action such as this a sin according to our religion, Islam? To this question, I have only the following answer: since I was a little girl at school, I have always been taught that the Prophet Muhammad, God bless his name, told his followers who were about to go to battle: Never cut down a tree, never kill a woman or child, never hurt an old man. In war, you should only kill warriors.

However, perhaps you already know that there are those who say that everyone in Israel counts as a warrior, because the children will grow up and go to the army, the women go to the army, and even some older men still do reserve duty. So there are those who would say: you are all warriors fighting us, the Palestinians, and therefore we are allowed to target you all.

To the third question: can there be any positive results to an action like this? the answer is that it is a tragedy for both sides. Innocent people have lost their lives, and the family of the man who did it will also suffer. His children will grow up fatherless, and who knows what else the future has in store for them. After each such incident, there is a curfew on our territories and on the Palestinians who are already suffering, and it makes us feel very helpless and hopeless. We lose even more of our simple daily rights, and we feel more and more suffocated.

So what is the solution, my friend? Do we need a miracle? Or do we just need someone to bring us together and to mediate? Or perhaps all those who try to bring us together and mediate are one of the causes of the problems?

The bottom line is that I have endless questions, endless question marks. Perhaps my letters to you will help me express some of them, and release some of the pressure that I've been feeling all my life.

The simple fact that I am able to tell you about my feelings, Daniela, can help. The fact that you are one of those people I always thought were the only obstacle on the way to my freedom, and that I can communicate with you like this, can help. Perhaps it will help change things, at least in my head.

My heart thumps every time a letter from you arrives, so please don't let me wait long.

Kisses to you and your family,
Shireen

July 10th, 2008
Ramallah

Dear Daniela,

I still haven't received your reply to the letter I sent you last week, but I did get a letter from you more than two weeks after you'd sent it, and it was open. I don't want to even try and guess who opened it and why, but I just want to say that it isn't right.

Now, to a different issue. Where do you come up with these accusations about our schoolbooks? When I went to

21

school, twenty-something years ago, there was nothing that taught us to hate Jews and Israelis in our schoolbooks, and there isn't anything like this today.

The European Union funds our schoolbooks these days, and when the rumours started in the media about hostile texts in the books, there was a special EU committee that looked into it. They found nothing.

So maybe it is time you understood that there are those who've got an interest to poison *your* minds against us, and the media is making a feast of it.

The only thing that makes our children hate Israelis is the occupation, and you Israelis have got the power to change that.

You probably never read the Holy Koran, but it teaches us to be tolerant towards all religions. Those who interpret it differently are simply wrong; even if they are our Muslim brothers and even if they are Palestinian.

Deep inside, we Palestinians are a modest and peaceful people. If something turned us hostile and violent, it was not the texts in our schoolbooks, but what we and our children see and endure every day.

Every time we have to wait for hours at a road-block – in the sun, wind or rain, only to go from town to town, or to visit relatives – something breaks inside us. I won't even mention those who have to reach a hospital or Palestinian women who are forced to give birth at road-blocks. How can a people like yours, who know what suffering is, make other people suffer so much?

But let's leave politics for now. I'd like to share with you an experience I had when we visited Geneva, and that I often think of. One Sunday, when it was particularly hot, we decided to go to a swimming pool in Nyon, about twenty minutes from Geneva. It was the most beautiful swimming pool I've ever seen; built right on Lake Geneva. From the main entrance it looks as if the swimming pool and the lake are one.

There is also a toddling pool and a restaurant, and large patches of grass. And one other thing: a small beach, with pebbles and a bit of sand, and a small wooden deck from which the kids could jump into the lake and swim in the shallow water. Of course, we have nothing like it in Palestine.

Saif and Ghazal were so excited about everything that they tried swimming in the lake, but gave up the idea when they felt how cold the water was. But me, I'd never swum in a lake in my life, and I was determined to try.

So I swam in the lake, and I enjoyed the experience very much, but it also made me feel sad – and it still makes me sad when I think of it today. Do you know why?

Because every time I think of that experience, I also think of my siblings and my friends here who have never experienced such a simple pleasure – of driving twenty minutes to a beautiful swimming pool without anyone stopping you and asking you where you are going and why. I will finish here. Please write soon.

Yours,
Shireen

★　★　★

July 10th, 2008
Tel Aviv

Dear Shireen,

I hope you and your family are well.

I was deeply touched by your last letter. Of course you don't hold any personal responsibility for what that man did in Jerusalem, and I don't expect you to be able to explain why he did it.

Getting on a tractor and running over people – innocent men, women and children – is such a horrific and inexplicable act that I don't think it is possible to understand it.

But I would like to ask you one thing: how can his mother, who has given birth to him and raised him and probably loved him very much, rejoice that her son did something so horrendous? How can she say he is a *shaiid*, a martyr? How can she not see that his act is insane and barbaric?

I read many articles about this incident, and also many of the reactions and comments that Israelis posted on the internet. There was one reaction that was repeated several times, and please forgive me for quoting it because it certainly does not reflect on you, but it was comparing Arab mothers with Jewish mothers.

"What is the difference between a Jewish mother and an Arab mother?" someone asks, and then goes on to reply: "That a Jewish mother mourns the loss of a child, and an Arab mother celebrates it."

24

"Of course, they have so many children," another wrote. "That when they lose one, it doesn't matter so much."

Of course, these are simplistic, generalising and cruel comments. But still, they reflect what people think. So maybe you can help me understand, how can a mother celebrate such a horrific act committed by her son? What in her culture (and I deliberately do not write "your culture") allows her to have such a reaction? How can the family build a hut and celebrate the son's death and martyrdom?

And even if this terrorist was an Israeli-Arab, and not a Palestinian from the Palestinian territories, and even if he had reasons to be upset (because it is certainly true that no one can commit such an act without having so much anger that they can't contain it), and even if a quarter of a million residents of East Jerusalem don't see themselves as part of the Jewish state and are not voting for parliament, and if they are absent from their homes for a certain period of time – even for studies or personal reasons – they will lose their status. Still.

How can anyone sane say that he did something positive? And that he is a *shaiid*? I am not even sure I completely understand what a *shaiid* is – is it someone who did something so wonderful that he'll go straight to heaven? And if so, how can anyone say that this madman was a *shaiid*?

Please forgive me, this is not a particularly positive letter, but I will try to end it on a positive note: my son Ben saw the pictures you've sent me, and he remembered meeting you and your kids in Geneva. You won't believe

25

what he said to me last night before he went to sleep. He pointed at a picture and said: "Shireen is my best friend." I am sure he remembers that you played with him and gave him lots of attention. I was amazed, but that was what he said, and it came straight from the heart.

I am waiting to hear from you – and please tell me more about your family. I would really like to be able to understand you better.

Daniela

★   ★   ★

July 20th, 2008
Ramallah

Dear Daniela,

I was delighted to receive your letter, which arrived relatively quickly this time – maybe it encountered fewer road-blocks on the way . . .

My husband walked in, shuffling the stack of paper in his hands, and pulled it out. He knows how excited I am every time a letter from you arrives.

I took it from him, and tore the envelope open while I was setting the table for dinner. I just couldn't wait. I must admit that I didn't read it properly the first time, because I was surrounded by hungry mouths. But then, at the end of the day, I sat quietly and read it again.

My little family and I, we are well, thank you for asking. As for my extended family, my mother is on a trip to Amman, Jordan, with my grandfather. They are visiting relatives.

Do you know, my dear, that the distance between Nablus and Amman is ninety kilometres, just over an hour's drive if there were no road-blocks? But of course, the road-blocks are there. So they left Nablus at five in the morning, and reached Amman at five in the afternoon. Twelve hours on the road. I called my mother to ask if they arrived safely, because my grandfather is eighty-eight years old. She said they were well, though exhausted.

Now to your letter and the questions in it. I will try to answer them as honestly as I can, because they are very important questions.

My dear, you asked how a mother can rejoice at her son's killing not only of himself, but also of others. Let me tell you the following: no mother in the world can rejoice in the loss of a son. If you could look deep into her eyes, you would see tears behind the mask she has put on. Of course she is saddened by the death of her son, the same son with whom she surely spent many sleepless nights.

But you know, according to our religion, this life is just the beginning. There is also the afterlife.

God gave us everything – our brains, our senses, our feelings, and he has also shown us the right path. But in the end, we are at liberty to make our own choices. We believe that it is in the afterlife that we shall be judged, by our actions in this life.

And evaluating our deeds in this life is neither in your hands, nor in mine. It is only in the hands of Allah.

Let's go back to what happened earlier this month in Jerusalem. This young man's mother probably believes that this life is only temporary, and that she will soon see her son again. In Islam we say that it is better to read a chapter of the Koran than to cry over the dead. Because what good will crying do?

This brings me to your second question – what is a *shaiid*, a martyr?

I don't want to go into too much detail, because this is a complex matter and, of course, I cannot say who is a *shaiid* and who isn't. This is in the hands of God. But I *can* tell you that a *shaiid* is someone who ends their life for a noble cause.

For example, a *shaiid* can be someone who was killed on their way to their studies, as well as someone who died in the line of duty, such as policemen, firemen, and even doctors and teachers. They will all be considered *shaiids*, if they die performing their duties.

Those who die in war are also considered *shaiids*, and the same goes for someone who has been fighting for their faith.

I know that you are now thinking: if your religion says not to kill women and children, how can someone who did still be considered a *shaiid*?

It is very difficult for me to answer this question, but I will do my best.

I believe in resistance to the occupation and to the soldiers who represent it. And you must understand that actions against your civilians are merely reactions to what is being done to ours, women and children included.

In order to resolve this problem, we need to stop the violence on both sides. Is this really so complicated, or are we the ones complicating things? When I say 'we', I mean both sides, of course.

You said that someone wrote a comment on the internet, claiming that since we have large families, it is less painful for us to lose a child. My dear, does this make any sense to you, a mother of two young boys? You think it would be different if you had more children? If, God forbid, you lost one of your children, would it be less painful because you had more than one child? Losing a child is always terrible, regardless of how many children you have.

As for the so-called celebration you mentioned – of the family who lost their son in Jerusalem – it is not a celebration at all. It is just a gathering of family and friends who have come to mourn. They do build a special hut for this gathering, but it is only because when someone dies, especially in these circumstances, people come from far and wide to support the family, and there is not room for everyone inside the house.

Now that I've answered your questions to the best of my ability, I have some questions of my own – and most of them come as a result of your questions.

Do you Israelis really think that we Palestinians are all cruel criminals? Don't you believe in our right to our own state? How do your people see mine? What do you think of us?

I must end here, because my children are fighting in the kitchen. I better go and make peace . . .

I hope my letter finds you and your family in good health.

Shireen

★ ⚜ ★

July 30th, 2008
Tel Aviv

Dear Shireen,

I thank you for the candid answers you gave in your last letter, even if I had trouble stomaching some of them. Your explanations help, and some things that seemed totally inexplicable before are a bit clearer now. Even if I disagree with some of the things that you wrote, an open dialogue is important as a first step.

You asked if we, Israelis, think of all Palestinians as cruel criminals. The short answer is obvious: of course not. But there are some who believe that there is no point in discussing things with you, because you see things very differently, and the interests of our two peoples are contradictory.

I personally believe that this is exactly the reason why we *should* be talking, to try and bridge the gaps that sometimes seem so unbridgeable.

However, there is a longer answer, and it is that after all the cruel terrorist attacks of the past two decades, many Israelis simply don't trust you. It is also true that parents teach their children that if they see someone suspicious, they should walk away. And unfortunately, this 'someone suspicious' would, most of the time, be Palestinian.

I agree, this is terrible. But please tell me: how many Israeli suicide bombers have you had in your areas over the past two decades?

Of course, it is impossible to deny that we did, and still are doing, some pretty awful things. I am sure you will say that since we've got tanks and guns, we don't need suicide bombers, and I can understand your point.

But please allow me to answer your question with a question: there are many who have suffered, and are suffering in this world. I am referring to entire people. And without undermining the importance or amount of Palestinian suffering, I am sure you know that there are many who have got much less than you, Palestinians – people in Africa, Latin America, even in Eastern Europe. And still, the suicide bomber phenomenon is much more prominent in the Middle East, and on this piece of land which we've been fighting over for the past sixty years. How come?

You asked if we don't believe in your right to a state. My answer to that is that actually, we do, and we did so even in 1948, when the UN made the declaration which divided the mandatory land of Palestine into the state of Israel for the Jewish people and the state of Palestine for the Palestinian people.

Please forgive me for being so direct, but it is the Palestinians and Arab countries who did not agree with this UN resolution and went to war.

And if we hadn't been attacked by the Arab armies in 1948, and if your people had recognised the state of Israel and the right of the Jewish people to their state back then, perhaps we would not have had reasons (as well as excuses) to make your lives miserable for the past sixty years. Not only that, but your Palestinian State could have been larger than it is today, after sixty years of wars and bloodshed.

31

It is true that neither you, nor any of those in our generation, were around in 1948, and maybe not even in 1967, when the Arab armies attacked Israel again and when this cursed occupation began. But what can we do? As the saying goes, 'The sons bear the sins of the fathers.' So your suffering, which I cannot deny exists, is not only the result of the Israeli occupation, but also the result of decisions your people made more than sixty years ago.

I wish there was a way to turn back time – I am convinced that both our people would have done some things differently!

But back to reality and present times. Not only do we believe in your right to a state, but there are many Israeli 'leftists' who even fight for your right to a state. But every Palestinian attack, and every missile that is launched from Gaza into southern Israel, and every extreme speech in the media and at the Friday prayers in the mosques, are weakening our 'peace front' and serve only those who do not want peace; who are interested in the continuation of the occupation; who did not renounce their dream of 'a greater Israel'. And those are the few, but also the most vocal, among us.

Most of us really would like to live beside you in peace, and believe that free, prosperous neighbours will also be good neighbours, who will mind their own business. And even if not every last Israeli believes that we could live alongside the Palestinians in friendship and tranquillity, most of us believe that we could live in separation, as long as there is peace and security for us.

And when there is security for us, you will profit from it, too – or at least I'd like to believe that this is the way things are. Do you really think that eighteen or nineteen year olds, or reservists who have families and other obligations, enjoy standing at road-blocks and checking Palestinian IDs and vehicles? They only do it because they believe it is a necessity for the security of their own families.

Ok, this is probably enough for today . . . Please write soon.

Yours,
Daniela

★ ★ ★

August 6th, 2008
Ramallah

Daniela,

Your last letter made me think, and ask myself many questions about what happened sixty years ago. I guess it is the same for you, but most of the information I get is from society around me, and from older people who can tell me what happened sixty years ago, in 1948.

Perhaps I should have been interested and asked more questions in the past, but I am asking them now. I searched for more information on the internet, mostly on what exactly happened in 1948. I have to say that I was surprised by some of the things I found.

When I read what you wrote about us not accepting the founding of the State of Israel in 1948, and that a lot of what happened thereafter was because of that, I gave it a lot of thought. But Daniela, do you really think that we, Palestinians, were in a situation where we could make our own decisions back then?

Do you know, my dear, that there were no more than 500 Palestinians who fought you back then? You were well organised and ready for war, with aid from the Americans and the British. Your *Hagana* organisation was well trained, while the Arab armies were scattered and quite disorganised, and it was the British who controlled the supply of weapons to the area.

And in the end, who was the side that really lost? Us, Palestinians. We lost our homes and our land. I tried to ask older relatives about what happened back then, and they all said that nobody asked them for their opinion. They were chased away from their homes and many of them were slaughtered in the war. Ever since, we have been waiting to have our own state.

My friend, the pain I see in my grandfather's eyes every time he talks about the house he built in Ramle with his own two hands is awful. I don't want him to die without seeing his dream for an independent Palestinian State come true. He told me that many years ago, when things were different, he passed by his old house, and stopped to knock on the door. A pleasant-looking woman opened it, and he told her that he used to live in that house, and that he would only like to see it one more time. She invited him in.

He accepted the invitation and looked around, only to see that not much had changed since he lived there. Of course he was sad to see the house that he built, but the visit also helped him accept the situation.

I hope this helps you, as well as me, to understand better what really happened back in those days. And perhaps it will help me change the image that we have in your eyes, a little bit.

Yours,
Shireen

★　★　★

August 7th, 2008
Tel Aviv

Dear Shireen,

I only received your letter from July 10th yesterday, and when I read it I felt a lump in my throat.

I know that swimming pool in Nyon very well, because we also went there when we were in Switzerland. Who knows, perhaps we were even there at the same time? It really is the nicest swimming pool I've ever seen, but here in Israel we have nice swimming pools, too. And despite the fact that it's very crowded because the kids are on their summer holiday and it is so hot that everyone is looking for a way to cool down, we go swimming almost every day. I wish you could come with us.

But you know very well that there were not always walls and road-blocks, and you told me yourself that when you were little you visited Natanya without any problems. So why are things different today? Not only because of us, but also because of you. Not you personally, of course, but I am sure you know what I mean.

Before the suicide bombings and the terror, you could come and work here, and visit, and no one told you what to do and what not to do. Perhaps this description is a bit rosy, and of course you were not exactly honorary citizens of the State of Israel, but still . . . If you had recognised the State of Israel when it was founded, or even a few years later, and if the radical Islamists hadn't taken over Gaza, and if and if and if . . . Then it is quite probable that you could have just gotten into your car right now and driven to Tel Aviv to join us on a visit to the swimming pool this afternoon.

I want you to know that people here do care about you. When you had internal conflicts in Gaza a few days ago, 150 Palestinians were allowed into Israel for humanitarian reasons, and at the request of the president of the Palestinian Authority. Then, when he asked that they be returned to Gaza (if I understand correctly, this was because they didn't want it to appear as if Fatah was abandoning Gaza), there were those who went to the Supreme Court in Israel and demanded that they not be returned, because they feared for their lives. So now they are sending them to Jericho. So you see, we do care.

Now to a different theme. I am very curious about the relationships between Muslims and Christians in your society. Are you friends? Do you intermarry? Do the Christians object to the existence of the State of Israel as strongly as the Muslims do?

I am sure you know that in Israel today there are more than a million Palestinians; Christians and Muslims. We, of course, like to call them 'Israeli Arabs'. And although I am sure they don't have a particularly easy life here, at least they have more freedom and more influence than you do. And I will not be hypocritical and try to pretend that they have complete equality in Israeli society, but it is a fact that there are Israeli Arabs who are ministers and members of parliament, and many others in positions of influence. There is even an Israeli Arab who is representing Israel as an ambassador with the Ministry of Foreign Affairs. Do you think there could ever be a Jewish minister in your government?

So you can see that not everything is our fault, and every story has more than one angle, as we like to say. One thing is for sure, both of us are paying the price for the mistakes that have been made in the past. The questions I ask myself every day now are: How long are we going to continue paying this price? And when does this price become too heavy to bear?

Yours,
Daniela

P.S. I am enclosing a present for Ghazal's birthday – a book titled "Uzo and Muzo from Kakaruzo". It is a translation from the Hebrew of a book by Israeli author Ephraim Sidon. My kids love listening to this story, and I hope that your kids will enjoy it, too. I looked long and hard for the Arabic translation, and in the end I had to go to Haifa, to a specialist shop where they stock Israeli books in Arabic translations.

★   ★   ★

37

Daniela Norris and Shireen Anabtawi

August 15th, 2008
Ramallah

Dear Daniela,

My children look at the picture of you and your boys on our fridge often, and ask when we will see you again. I don't know what to tell them.

Thank you for the book you sent for Ghazal, about Uzo and Muzo. She saw when I took it out of the envelope and refused to wait for her birthday – she asked me to read it to her immediately. So far, I've read it about ten times. There is something very familiar about this story . . .

A couple of days ago I went to a party at one of my friend's houses. It was a girls' night, and we all dressed up for it. We took some pictures, and I will send you a couple, so you can see some of my best friends. We live in different places – some in towns, some in villages. And some are Muslims, others are Christians.

It was a wonderful evening. We got some peace and quiet from our children and our husbands. We listened to music and laughed a lot. And of course, we ate delicious food.

Before I get into telling you about the differences between Muslims and Christians in our society, I would like to say that when I was little and able to visit all the nice places you mentioned, we were still under occupation. Despite the fact that we had more freedom and could move around and travel, we were still occupied, and therefore not content. This, of course, is why the *intifada* started.

You've asked about the difference between Palestinian Muslims and Christians. You've asked if the Christians also

38

resist the occupation. My answer to this is that there is no real difference between us. We are all the sons and daughters of the same land, and we all suffered and will continue to suffer until we have our own state. As for marriage – there are many successful marriages between Palestinian Muslims and Christians (though mostly done against the will of the families . . .). Of course, there are ones that fail – as with all marriages. We have the same customs, we eat the same food, and our children go to the same schools. We are neighbours and colleagues.

What about you and the Palestinians who live in Israel? Can you be friends? Are there Christians who are Israeli citizens? And how do the rights of Jewish Israelis and non-Jewish Israelis differ? (I know you have said there are differences . . .)

My daughter goes to summer camp this year – I signed her up so she can have the chance to have fun with other kids her age. They take them swimming, dancing, to the cinema. As for Saif, he is a very active little boy . . . he goes to kindergarten every day from eight to three – even in the summer. Of course, even in the summer I have to work every day! But in a few days I'm taking a week off, and I'll take both my kids to visit my parents in Nablus. What about you? What are your kids doing this summer?

I sometimes feel that we are interrogating each other. Every letter contains more and more questions, but the answers to these questions help us understand each other better. This is something we couldn't do before we met – despite the fact that we have lived on the same piece of land for so many years.

I cannot end this letter without mentioning that last week we lost our national poet, Mahmoud Darwish. He is the one who wrote many of the songs we sing and poems we recite at our schools and universities. He died at the age of sixty-seven, after a failed heart-operation in the United States. Not very long ago I saw him here in Ramallah, eating at a restaurant called Villa Vachi. It's a great place, which we call *La Hakura*, the yard. The food is served in the courtyard, around a swimming pool, and they specialise in *fuhara*, food cooked in clay pots. The owner is Armenian, and I hope we can go there together one day for dinner.

The fact that I saw him there made his death even more shocking for me – but he will always continue to live in our hearts and minds, through his poems.

I hope to read your letter soon!

Kisses,
Shireen

August 20th, 2008
Nablus

Dear Daniela,

I hope that you and your family are well. We, thank God, are fine.

Yesterday I arrived in Nablus for a visit with my family, and I am writing to you from my parents' house. I will stay here a week, and spend some time with my mother.

I don't know if you realise what the condition of the roads between our towns is nowadays. In the past, it would take me forty minutes to get from Ramallah to Nablus.

These days, it can take anywhere between an hour-and-a-half and five hours (and even more, sometimes).

It's even sort of funny, because it is easier to get from Ramallah to Geneva than it is to get from Ramallah to visit my parents in Nablus. I would like to tell you about one of the adventures I had when I tried, one day, to get from Nablus to Ramallah. At the time, before I was married, I lived in Nablus and worked in Ramallah.

One day, I left my house in Nablus at five in the morning, as usual, to get to work in Ramallah at eight. There were seven of us, including myself and my cousin, and we shared the same taxi every morning and every evening.

That morning, the Hawara check-point was as crowded as it is every morning. But unlike every other morning, on that day they decided that no one could go through. Our taxi driver suggested that we drive through the hills and through the village 'Till, instead.

Normally we had another taxi driver waiting for us on the other side of the Hawara check-point to drive us on to Ramallah, because taxis from Nablus cannot cross to Ramallah and vice versa. It is not only taxis that are sanctioned – even private vehicles are not supposed to cross, except for a very few who have special permits.

Anyway, we wanted to get to work on time, and we accepted the driver's suggestion. We drove back a few hundred meters, and started driving towards 'Till on a dirt road. When we reached the village we had to get out of the car and walk, and in the meantime we called the driver of the other taxi and asked him to wait for us outside 'Till, instead of on the other side of Hawara. The only problem was that when the Occupation Forces learned that people sometimes use 'Till to cross between Ramallah and Nablus, they put an army post on top of the hill.

So our taxi reached the hill where we had to get out, and we put on our boots. We always carry walking boots with us, because we never know when we may have to walk in the mud. It was nearly six o'clock when we started walking. It had rained in the night, and the earth was very muddy.

Suddenly I heard a loud noise and when I looked around I saw everyone running. I turned and saw Israeli tanks approaching us from the hill where the army post was. We ran as fast as we could, trying to get to the taxi that waited for us on the other side of the village, before the tanks could reach and stop us.

Suddenly we heard the sound of a horn, and my cousin stopped running and looked around her, surprised.

"What's the matter?" I called towards her.

"I didn't know that tanks had horns!" she called back.

"Stop talking rubbish and just run!" I yelled.

We finally made it to the taxi that waited for us, but many others didn't make it, because the tanks drove faster than they could run. They had to walk back all the way to Hawara, and probably didn't make it to work in Ramallah that day. Actually, sometimes this can be a very good excuse. What can the boss say if his employees tell him they were chased by tanks?

I got into the taxi, panting, and tried to slow my breath down. Because we took the same taxi every morning, we were friendly with the driver, whose name was Bilaal. I will tell you more about him in the future.

CROSSING QALANDIYA

On that day, I was an hour late for work, but at least I made it. This is only one of many stories I could tell about my daily life, but now I must stop because my mother is upset that I am writing to you instead of talking to her. So I will leave you, my friend.

Yours,
Shireen

★   ★   ★

August 27th, 2008
Tel Aviv

Dear Shireen,

Many thanks for your two letters, which arrived a day apart, and helped me to picture your life a little better. It is so different from mine, despite the fact that we live such a small distance apart. Being chased by tanks on your way to work . . . what can I say? It sounds hallucinogenic, but I am sure you didn't make any of it up, and that you do indeed live a harsh reality. The one thing I can say is that I wish I could do something to change things.

Please tell your parents that your Israeli friend hopes to meet them one day – if they'd be interested in meeting me, that is.

You've asked whether we befriend the Palestinians who live in Israel, and whether members of all faiths have equal rights. The answers, in principle, are 'yes' and 'yes', but the real, honest answers are 'no' and 'not really' – judging by what I see around me.

A short while ago there was an article in one of the papers, discussing how our prime minister has announced that it is time to stop the discrimination against the Israeli Arabs. He said that the Israeli public should be educated to understand that Israeli Arabs are citizens with equal rights. This mere statement shows, of course, that they aren't. How does this manifest itself in daily life? In everything, really.

You may know that in Israeli society, a lot depends on what you did during your military service (and Israeli Arabs are exempt from military service, of course). For example, a man who spends his military service in a combat unit is usually seen as a brave fighter who is defending his country, while someone who spends their military service as a clerk or driver will not be as appreciated. But there are always special cases.

There is one Israeli Arab, a journalist, whom I really admire. His name is Sayed Kashua, and I read his column in *Haaretz* every Friday, before I look at anything else in the weekend edition of the paper.

With a lot of humour, he manages to express what the Arab citizens of Israel feel. He also created a very successful television series, in a similar vein. He wrote some funny things recently about the difficulties of trying to open a business bank account with an Arab name on your ID, and about how his family criticises him for trying to talk and dress like his Jewish neighbours.

What can you do? Sometimes you have to reach out and take your rights, and not wait until they are handed to you on a silver platter, especially in a state like ours. But you can demand your rights politely, not forcefully and, if possible, with a certain amount of humour – because it is a powerful way of getting a message across.

As I've written, the reality is far from ideal, but I do think we are on the right road – a road that recognises mistakes of the past and the fact that there are things in our society that need changing. We are a paranoid society, possibly because of things we've been through in our recent and not-so-recent history. Our paranoia causes us to be harsh. We are harsh towards others, harsh towards ourselves and, particularly, we are harsh towards you, Palestinians.

But we must give each other a chance to fix past mistakes – we have no other choice!

Yours,
Daniela

★   ★   ★

September 4th, 2008
Ramallah

My friend,

I am writing to you now, and it is nearly midnight. What can I do? It is the only time I can get to myself. My days are taken over by all my duties, and there are days when I can't even find time to look in the mirror.

It is quite amusing when I remember what my mother used to tell me when I was younger: "Enjoy your days now, my daughter," she used to say. "Enjoy it while you are being spoiled. It will not always be like this."

Daniela Norris and Shireen Anabtawi

Now I understand what she meant.

Thank you for your last letter. I really appreciate your frankness. I learn a lot from each one and – surprisingly – I even find myself agreeing with some of the things you write.

It still smells of onions in this room because I cooked a traditional Palestinian meal earlier, and that is its main ingredient. I promise I will make it for you one day.

You are probably curious to know what it is – but I'm not sure I am allowed to tell you this secret . . . Just joking, of course! Here's the recipe:

You'll need to use quite a few onions. I am sure that's easy to find in Tel Aviv. You'll also need some olive oil, which you're probably not short of either. The other ingredients are chicken, thinly sliced almonds and pita bread. You can serve it with yogurt and finely chopped cucumber, tomato and parsley salad– what we call an Arab salad – seasoned with lemon juice and maybe some coriander.

Start by boiling the chicken in a big pot of water, but don't leave it too long, or it will get soggy. When it's about half-cooked, take out the chicken and put it in the hot oven, roasting until golden-brown. In the meantime, you can start chopping the onions and stir-frying them in a frying-pan. When they've turned a bit golden, cover them with olive oil, and add some salt to the mixture. Cook for ten to fifteen minutes while stirring.

Then you'll have to add a tangy purple spice called *sumac*, which I am pretty sure you use in your cooking. It is a spice used in many kinds of Arab food, and you won't find an Arab kitchen that doesn't have it in stock.

Put quite a lot of *sumac* on the onion mixture, and then tip in all into a large bowl. Take a piece of pita bread, fold it in two and dip it in the olive oil. Wring the olive oil out and spread the pita on an oven tray. Put a couple on spoonfuls of the onion on each piece of pita bread. Then fry the sliced almonds and put some of this on the pita bread too, and you're nearly done. When the chicken is well cooked, chop it into pieces and serve with the pita bread with onions and almonds, and the yogurt and Arab salad side-dishes. Enjoy!

Writing all this has made me hungry again, but I won't eat a crumb as it is too late for eating. But my dear, in exchange for this secret recipe, I expect one of yours in your next letter . . .

I feel my eyes starting to close, so I will end here. I hope you enjoy my recipe.

Kisses,
Shireen

★ ★ ★

September 10th, 2008
Tel Aviv

Dear Shireen,

Thank you for the recipe you sent in your last letter. I thought of trying to make it, but then I decided to wait. I hope that in the not-too-distant-future I will be able to come and eat it at your house – and I am sure it would be much more pleasant and tasty than any culinary attempt on my part!

You've asked for one of our recipes. Well, at the end of the month we celebrate the New Year, five-thousand-seven-hundred-sixty-nine. We count the years since the creation of the world, and usually celebrate the Jewish New Year's Eve with a multi-course family dinner. As I am not a great cook, instead of giving you a recipe, perhaps I will describe to you what we eat for this traditional dinner. This, of course, changes slightly from home to home and from family to family.

We normally start with chicken soup. It is usually clear with some cooked carrots and parsley floating inside, and some people also serve *krepalah*, which are a sort of delicious dumpling with a bit of minced meat stuffing.

For the main course, it can be roast chicken or beef, with lots of vegetables and various salads. For some reason, there is always more on the table than anyone can ever dream of eating. I guess it symbolises plenty.

For dessert our family will usually eat fruit salad – either fresh or cooked. If it's a cooked fruit salad, then the fruit is boiled in water with sugar and cinnamon, and some red wine for those who like it. The fruit absorbs the water and swells, exploding with the mixture of sweet water-and-wine sauce. It is the most wonderful thing on a cool September evening.

Other than all that I have described, there is also some traditional food-stuff on the New Year's dinner table. These items are used for ceremonial purposes, but we do eat some of them, too. For example, there will always be the head of a fish, which symbolises the wish to become a head and not a tail in the coming year. There will also be pomegranate seeds, which symbolise the many good deeds we wish to perform.

The period between the New Year and Yom Kippur, the Jewish Day of Atonement, is a period where Jews reflect on the past year, on all the good and bad things they've done, and on how they can improve in the New Year.

It is a time when we are supposed to ask for forgiveness for all the sins we've committed, and apologise to those we have hurt or offended. Then, when we fast on Yom Kippur, we are atoning for all these sins. Religious people believe that God can forgive the sins they've committed, if they atone properly . . .

I already know, my friend, what I will be thinking of this coming Yom Kippur. Despite the fact that I don't have direct responsibility for the situation, I certainly feel that I have somewhat of a collective responsibility!

Yours,
Daniela

*   *   *

September 17th, 2008
Ramallah

My dear friend,

I was very glad to receive your last letter and learn about some of your customs and traditions. I really like the idea of the head of the fish – maybe I will adopt it!

We are now in the month of Ramadan, which came this year in parallel to the beginning of the new school year, because – as I am sure you know – it is decided by a lunar calendar and the date changes every year.

My daughter Ghazal is very happy to go back to school. It is the same school she has gone to since she was four, but this year she starts primary school, so she will be in the bigger section. This year the real work will begin.

I bought her a new school bag, books and pencils, and she is very excited about it all. This year she will also start learning French (because she goes to a private school – Rahabat Maar Yusuf – Saint Joseph School). She can hardly wait to start, because she picked up a few words when we visited Switzerland, and likes to practise them.

I am not sure how much you know about Ramadan, so I will tell you a little about our customs during this month.

During Ramadan we fast from sunrise to sunset, in order to feel closer to God. It also helps us identify with the poor, who don't always have food on the table, and it is healthy, because the body is cleansed from all the toxins.

We start the *iftar*, the first meal we take in the day, after sunset, by eating dates. Then we traditionally eat some soup and salad, and then the rest of the meal.

The most important things in the month of Ramadan are praying and reading the Holy Koran. But this doesn't mean that we can't enjoy some delicious sweets that are made especially during Ramadan, called *atayef*.

Sometimes we also nibble something before sunrise, perhaps a date or a small piece of cake, and we drink a glass of milk or some juice, because the prophet Muhammad said that this would bless the fast of that day.

CROSSING QALANDIYA

I wish you could come and visit me in the month of Ramadan, so you could feel the special atmosphere, especially towards the end of the month, during the *Eid el Fiter*.

One of the most important duties for men during this month is keeping in touch with their female relatives: their mothers, sisters and cousins. We always invite family and friends to break the fast together in the evenings, and it turns this month into a time of real family bonding.

During Ramadan we work shorter hours, and the kids study for fewer hours at school, too. This, of course, makes them very happy.

All the adults and adolescents must fast, though there isn't a set date for young people to start fasting. Girls will start fasting the year they get their period, and boys when they start growing facial hair. Of course, they can fast before this, and there are many children who start the day fasting and then eat before sunset, before the adults do.

It's really amusing that Ghazal, who is only six, is very happy to try and fast, because she doesn't like eating. As for my husband, the only thing that bothers him is not being able to smoke during the day.

You can't begin to imagine the traffic jams just before sundown, when everyone is trying to get home in time for dinner! And only minutes after sunset, the streets are silent. The only sound you can hear is the clanking of the knives and forks inside the homes.

And because during the day when the women are cooking for the evening meal everyone can smell the fragrant dishes being prepared, just before sundown the tradition is that neighbours bring each other a taste of what they've cooked – so everyone shares their neighbours' food.

I hope I have not bored you with my tales of Ramadan! I think this is enough for today, and don't forget that you are invited to come to my house for Ramadan dinner, if not this year then the next, *inshallah*.

Kisses,
Shireen

*   *   *

September 27th, 2008
Tel Aviv

Hello Shireen,

Many thanks for your interesting letter. I always heard people talk of Ramadan, and knew that Muslims fast during this month, but never understood exactly what it was all about. The details are fascinating.

You may also have heard of our Yom Kippur high holiday which I mentioned in my last letter. This year it will be on October 8th, and it is similar to your Ramadan in many ways. Firstly, the atmosphere in Israel during Yom Kippur is very special. Despite the fact that not everyone fasts, as there are many secular Israelis, we all feel the special meaning of the day. Those who fast normally also go to the synagogue to pray, and some take to the streets – which are free of traffic – for a stroll around their neighbourhood.

The children and young people take advantage of the fact that there are no cars on the roads, and they all take their bicycles and rollerblades out onto the streets in the evening. You already know that I am a secular Jew, and in secular society many use this day of rest and reflection to meet friends and neighbours, read books or watch videos and DVDs. Of course, the religious Jews don't do this – they don't even light a fire, or turn on any reading lights or electrical appliances – just like on the Saturday, the Sabbath, but even stricter.

We do have an age when children become adults and therefore start to perform their religious duty if they choose – girls become women at twelve, and this is celebrated in a Bat-mitzvah ceremony, and boys become men at thirteen, after their Bar-mitzvah.

Some celebrate the Bar-mitzvah in a synagogue, or have a big party, and others use it as an excuse to take a family trip abroad or just celebrate with close friends and classmates, or even go to the Wailing Wall, the last remaining wall of the Second Temple in Jerusalem.

When we met, I told you that I lived abroad for quite a few years. I find it interesting that when I did live outside Israel, I felt more of a need to observe Yom Kippur, because I missed the holiday atmosphere which we all take for granted here as part of our culture. What happens if you are abroad during Ramadan – doesn't it make it more difficult for you to fast if everyone around you is eating and drinking?

And as we are discussing holidays, I better start preparing for Rosh Hashanah, the Jewish New Year, which we celebrate the day after tomorrow, on Monday night. We won't be celebrating it at our house – I already told you that I am not an enthusiastic cook and prefer to eat my

53

mother's food, which is excellent. So this year we'll celebrate Rosh Hashanah at my mum's house, with my brother and some uncles and cousins. We'll be twelve in total – I don't have a big family, as both my mother and father are only children.

Because my mum is remarried and her husband is my second father (with all love and respect to my wonderful biological father), I consider his family as my family, despite the fact that there is no blood relation. He has a brother and a sister whom I like very much, and we often celebrate the holidays with them and their families.

Well, I don't want to bore you with the details – so I will end here and wait for your letter. Like we say here in Israel – 'tzom kal' – have an easy fast.

Yours,
Daniela

★   ★   ★

October 15th, 2008
Ramallah

Dear Daniela,

Let me start by inquiring about your and your family's health. We are fine, thank God. I didn't reply to your letter immediately this time, because I have been busy with the *Eid el Fiter* celebrations.

You know, before I met you and your family, I always thought of all Israelis as enemies. Now it's different. Now that I see you as simply people, I regard you in a much more humane way. The process I went through is very strange for me, my dear. If I try to think of it logically and consider our case, I reach the conclusion that all we really need is better communication. We have to find a solution, because so few people realise just how much this could change their daily lives.

I don't know why, but this is the first time since we started corresponding that I'm finding it difficult to write to you. I've been holding my pen for nearly an hour, and nothing is coming out. Perhaps it is because I have so much to say to you.

So now I will tell you about what we did over the four days of *Eid el Fitr*. On the first day of the holiday, most people go to their grandparents' homes for breakfast. Since I got married, we always go to my mother-in-law's house, as she is the grandmother of my children. Traditionally, the following day we will visit my parents' house.

On the first day of the *Eid* we eat a festive breakfast – things like liver and salty fish. Of course, the greatest pleasure of that morning is the coffee, after not having our morning coffee for an entire month during Ramadan! That for me is the most difficult part of the month-long fast.

Fasting during Ramadan helps us appreciate things we normally don't think about; like this daily cup of coffee; like the glass of water we don't even think about drinking mid-morning; like having something to eat during the day.

During the *Eid* everyone wears new clothes and children get presents – toys and sweets. The men are usually the ones who buy and distribute these gifts, and they also give the children *Eid*-money, which we call '*Eidia*'. So we are all dressed in our best clothes, receiving presents – and the men are the ones who have all the worries. My husband always jokes that men don't benefit much from this holiday!

My mother-in-law also cooks lunch – she'll prepare things like vegetables stuffed with meat and rice, *tabule*, a kind of salad, *kube*, which is like a meatball, and many kinds of salads. After lunch, my husband, his father and his brothers leave the house and visit family, friends and neighbours. Each visit may last only a few minutes – but the main thing is to go and pay respects to everyone.

One other thing made especially for the *Eid* are cakes called *maamul* (which means 'made' in Arabic) and I absolutely adore them. For your information, during each and every *Eid* I put on at least four pounds, because I like these cakes so much!

So today I am embarking on a diet to try and lose the extra weight. What about you? Do you also gain weight during the holidays? And how is little Ben – have you managed to potty-train him?

I better finish here, because it is 1:30am and in just a few hours I need to get up for school and work.

Kisses,
Shireen

★   ★   ★

October 20th, 2008
Tel Aviv

Hello Shireen,

Thanks so much for your last letter, and for all the holiday stories. I really feel like I am getting to know you and your people better. It's funny that we are both in a holiday period. This week we celebrate *Sukot* – tabernacles. It is one of the three *regalim*; the biblical pilgrimage festivals, when Jews would pilgrimage to the Temple in Jerusalem.

We celebrate this holiday to commemorate the people of Israel who lived in huts when they left Egypt and travelled through the Sinai desert. I am sure you already know a little about our history: the people of Israel were slaves in Egypt, and the prophet Moses (who, if I am not mistaken, you also believe in?) led them out of Egypt through the desert for forty years, and into the promised land of Israel. Of course, this was all in coordination with God's will (please forgive my cynicism).

Observant Jews build their own huts during this festival, and eat and sometimes even sleep in them. Secular Jews, like myself, are happy just to visit other people's huts – only because it is fun – not because of religious reasons.

Kids love this holiday, because they enjoy decorating the huts with drawings, paper-chains and other decorations. And of course, like most holidays, they get presents!

But for many couples in Israel, the holiday issue is a painful one: which of the two families will they spend each holiday with?!

Fortunately in my family this is not a big deal, because no one puts pressure on us, but I have many friends who quarrel with their spouses over this, and the compromise is usually one holiday with one partner's family, the next with the other's. You know we live in a tiny country, so distance or travel-time is never really an excuse!

How is it with you? You said before that you choose to spend certain holidays at your in-laws' – are there rules on this? And I am also curious to know – what are relationships between families like in your society? When a couple marries, do the families become close and celebrate holidays together?

You know, we've been living such a small geographical distance from each other for such a long time that when we started corresponding, I suddenly felt as if I'd been living with my eyes covered for so many years. No one is to blame but me – I suppose it was my choice to ignore your existence and to believe everything that is said about your people. There are other Israelis who do ask questions, even difficult ones. They not only ask questions, but also fight so we can live side by side in peace. They are called *'smollanim'*- The Leftists. Sometimes this word is used as a swear-word in our society . . .

I never defined myself as "a Leftist", but if being one means that I am opening my eyes and facing reality, asking questions and admitting that perhaps you are a little bit right after all, then perhaps I am becoming one.

And perhaps I am an optimist, or maybe just naïve, but I would like to believe that if everyone knew some of what I know today after a few months of friendship with a Palestinian, then they would all care a little more about what happens on your side. This, of course, without undermining what is going on in Israel. I'm sure you are familiar with the cliché about there being two sides to every story, but in our case it seems that there are more than two sides. There's your side, my side, and then there's the truth, which is somewhere in the middle.

Ok, it looks like I'm getting into midnight philosophy, and I am sitting here with a glass of red wine at my side (I suspect you don't drink alcohol) which is making me feel somewhat drowsy. So I will go to bed now.

Please write soon.
Daniela

P.S. I am working on potty-training Ben . . . I've been very motivated since you told me that your Saif has been potty-trained since he was eighteen months old. Wish me luck!

★   ★   ★

October 27th, 2008
Ramallah

My Dear,

I feel the need to write to you, especially when I feel lonely here in Ramallah. I told you when we met that I was born and grew up in Nablus, and despite the fact that I've been living in Ramallah for seven years now and have many friends, Nablus still holds a very special place in my heart.

If my husband read this letter, he would probably be very annoyed with me. My connection to Nablus is a very sensitive subject in our household. Despite the fact we live in a small country, there is a big difference between the towns themselves, towns and villages in general and, of course, between towns, villages and refugee camps.

I was born and raised in a city, and our customs in Nablus are somewhat different from those in the rest of Palestine. I just love Nablus because of its beauty, its special architecture and the two mountains guarding it – Gerizim and Ebal. Most of the houses are old, and the city itself is ancient, but that's a good thing in my eyes, because you can practically smell its history.

Nablus is also well known for its extraordinary food, and for the close bond among its inhabitants. Some say that this bond is exaggerated – but the truth is that it can't be fully appreciated until you are away from Nablus. I miss it so much.

Life in Ramallah is strange. On one hand, the town has an almost European feel to it. On the other hand, it isn't really a city. It's a small town, full of foreigners. Most of the residents of Ramallah came from other places, and its original inhabitants are very few. The fact that it is relatively easy to get in and out of Ramallah – there are only a few check-points – leads many people to move here, and there are more opportunities for work and places to go out.

I know I can't live in Nablus at the moment. Life there is harsh, because of the closures and all the mess that is going on there. Every time I visit I hear gunshots all around, and there are constant confrontations between the army and the militants. But I still miss it, and I keep longing to be there.

My husband's family is relatively small, and only a few of them live in Ramallah. His extended family lives elsewhere, and there are not many family events. This is one thing I miss terribly.

Marcel Khalife, a Palestinian-Lebanese singer, has a song that expresses my feelings well. Some of the lyrics are: "I miss my mother, her coffee, her bread, her touch. I miss my childhood."

And since I mentioned music, I will send you a CD with some of my favourite songs. I know you won't understand the words, but at least you can listen to the melodies.

There are some other things I forgot to tell you about Nablus: it is known for many things, and three of these are *knafe* (a delicious dessert made from a traditional Nablus cheese), Nabulso soap and, lastly, its beautiful women . . . just joking. Actually, I am not!

It is also famous for its ancient Turkish baths. Unfortunately, some of them were destroyed by your missiles during the fighting. It is hard to lose such places, because they are part of our history. There are similar baths in Syria, but I would like to invite you one day to come with me to the Turkish baths in Nablus. I won't tell you much about the bathing ceremony because I want you to be curious and come and try it for yourself. But I will say that you come out feeling as smooth and radiant as a baby!

What else can I tell you?

Two days ago, a relative of one of my best friends was arrested on his way back from Jordan. I know him well – he is very cultured, with a gorgeous family. He is a businessman, and very wealthy, but his political affiliation is Hamas – which is probably why he was arrested.

My dear husband is already snoring next to me, and I have managed to ignore it until now because I was so concentrated in writing to you. But I should probably end here and hide the letter until I post it off tomorrow morning – I really don't want my husband to read it.

Good night,
Shireen

Daniela Norris and Shireen Anabtawi

* * *

November 5th, 2008
Tel Aviv

Hello Shireen,

I am so thrilled every time a letter from you arrives –
your lines always fill me with inspiration. Thank you for
the invitation to come with you to the Turkish baths in
Nablus – I would be delighted to come, when the situation
allows. I hope this will be soon.

I was saddened to read about the destroyed baths in
Nablus. We are always quick to criticise regimes and
people who do such things – and it is hard for me to
imagine that we are capable of it, too. I am sure that if we
check this thoroughly, we will find an explanation for what
happened. I almost wrote "excuse", but no – I prefer to
look for an explanation.

Yesterday was Yitzhak Rabin's Memorial Day and –
after many years of not going – I went to the ceremony at
the Rabin Square in Tel Aviv. It is a large square in the
centre of town, and he was shot there by a Jewish assassin
in 1995[3] – I am sure you know the tragic story.

My paternal grandparents, who both died a long time
ago, used to have an apartment just next to the square. They
bought it more than forty years ago, when the area was on
the outskirts of the city and instead of a large square there

---

3 Yitzhak Rabin was assassinated on November 4th, 1995 by right-wing Israeli
radical Yigal Amir, who was opposed to Rabin's signing of the Oslo Accords.
The shooting took place in the evening as Rabin was leaving a mass rally in Tel
Aviv in support of the Oslo process. Amir was sentenced to life imprisonment.

was a zoo. I spent many weekends with my grandparents, and I remember often waking in the morning to the trumpeting of elephants and the shrieks of monkeys.

When the windows were open and all the buildings around were only four storeys high, I could see the sea, and the most glorious sunsets. They painted the sky in a pinkish-purple colour which I haven't seen anywhere else in the world – and I have visited many places.

It is funny how our childhood memories can be so strong. There tend to be flavours and smells we can still recall decades later. I remember the flavour of the chicken soup my grandmother used to make – clear chicken soup with carrots and parsley. I always insisted that she take out the parsley, otherwise I'd push my plate away. I have never tasted such delicious chicken soup again since she died.

Back to Yitzhak Rabin and his assassination. I was twenty-something when it happened, and I wasn't very politically-minded. I only started caring after he was murdered. Of course, a couple of years after his assassination the situation deteriorated, and I am sure you know the script from there as well as I do. But I am curious to find out – what did people in Palestine think of his murder? And what do they say today?

I was very interested to read what you wrote about the towns and villages – I really didn't think there were such differences in your society. I must admit that until not very long ago I was quite ignorant about Palestinian culture, and since I've never had a Palestinian girl friend (and certainly not a Palestinian boyfriend) I have never really tried to find out more. Most things I knew, I learned from the media – and I am sure you can imagine how objective that is . . .

Please tell me more about your society, about your childhood in Nablus and your life in Ramallah – are those two cities really so different? When I hear the names "Nablus" and "Ramallah" in the news, it is usually regarding terrorists who were arrested or weapons that were confiscated. I am sure there is a lot more to these places than that! What is the atmosphere like? Where do people go out? Is it like Israel, with lots of restaurants, clubs and cinemas? Do you go out a lot at night, and is it easy to find someone to baby-sit your kids?

We haven't been going out much over the past few years, since our boys were born. I know the time for going out in the evenings will come again but, in the meantime, we are so tired at the end of the day that when we don't go to bed early we mostly have friends over or watch a DVD.

I was also sorry to read that your friend's relative was arrested, but I can't stop myself from asking the question . . . why was he arrested? Not that I am such an expert on the different factions in Palestinian politics, but I do know there is a big difference between Hamas and Fatah. Hamas are the radical ones, Fatah are the reasonable ones. Hamas doesn't recognise the right of Israel to exist, and Fatah does. Which is why we negotiate with Fatah, and not Hamas.

Ok, let's put politics aside for a while. I wanted to tell you that last weekend, because the weather was so gorgeous, we went to the Galilee, and when I looked at the Arab villages on the way, I saw them in a totally different light. I think it is the first time that I really paid attention, and I saw that there is good reason for the frustration among Israeli Arabs. Some of these villages looked quite neglected, especially in comparison with Israeli villages and towns.

Perhaps you'll recall that I told you about an Israeli-Arab journalist whom I admire. I recently bought and read a book he wrote some years back, and it was ages since a book has made me laugh and cry as much as his did. I am not sure whether it is supposed to be an autobiographical book, but the protagonist is an Arab-Israeli boy who grew up in one of the Arab villages in Israel and was accepted to an Israeli school for gifted children.

He describes the difficulties which this boy went through and the dilemmas he faced as an Arab in Israeli society. But you know what? If this little boy is him, then in the end it all paid off, because he is very successful now – and this proves what I have always believed: if you want to succeed, you have to work hard, even if the odds are against you.

So on this optimistic note I'll end my letter – apologies that it ended up being so long! And I await your next letter impatiently; I am hoping that it will help relieve some of the confusion that I experience so often nowadays.

Yours,
Daniela

*   *   *

November 16th, 2008
Ramallah

Dear Daniela,

The day you wrote me your last letter was exactly a week before the memorial day for the death of Abu Ammar – Yasser Arafat. It is really strange that these two leaders, who started the peace process and shook hands in Oslo, died on almost the same date. It was nine years after Rabin's assassination but still, commemorating both their deaths in November, a week apart, is quite strange.

I think that the death of Rabin was a great loss to us, Palestinians – perhaps even a greater loss than it was to you, Israelis. Because if he were alive today, maybe we would have found a solution to our problems by now. He was a good partner for peace for us – which, of course, is why he was murdered. I worry that we will not have such a good partner for peace again. And whether you like it or not, I don't think we will have a leader like Yasser Arafat again – a leader who is a symbol to us all, one who everyone respects and whose decisions everyone accepts.

But now to a different topic: you asked whether it is easy to find someone to look after our children when we go out at night. My usual baby-sitter is my neighbour, and she looks after them for free. If she can't baby-sit, then I'll ask her daughter to do it, but I insist on paying her. And if they are both busy, I ask my mother-in-law or sister-in-law. They are usually willing to help out.

We don't go out much – perhaps once or twice a month. When we do go out, it is usually to a restaurant or on special occasions such as weddings – the kind that children are not invited to! Sometimes we go out to dinner with my husband's work colleagues, or to friends' birthday parties and celebrations.

You've also asked me to tell you more about Nablus and Ramallah. This is a topic I can write about for hours, because I think about it almost every day. I already told you that my husband really dislikes it when I compare the two . . . but as you wrote in your letter, childhood memories are powerful. I can't help it. My childhood memories are from Nablus – the smells, the flavours, the people. And they are very different from the ones in Ramallah. I miss the feeling in Nablus of being one big family; the traditional coffee mornings, sharing an evening meal with neighbours . . .

I am sure you'll hear more from me about this in the future, but right now I have to go and do some shopping, and drag both kids with me. Wish me luck!

Yours,
Shireen

        ★ ★ ★

November 22nd, 2008
Tel Aviv

Hi Shireen,

Yes, childhood memories . . . it is very strange how some things get stuck in our heads.

These things make us see the world in a certain way, and then it becomes difficult to change these perceptions. One of the main problems in the relationship between our peoples is the new generation – a generation that grows up in a reality of conflict and hatred.

After all, you did tell me that from the moment your children learn to walk, they also learn to throw stones. And our children, from the moment they learn to talk and understand, they hear that there are Palestinians, and that they are dangerous. It's a terrible situation. What will we do now, with all these children – Israeli and Palestinian – who have learned to hate each other?

True, there are many programmes that try to bridge the gaps between the two sides. And some of these initiatives really do wonderful work, but the majority of people have no real knowledge of each other, and this is very unfortunate, and dangerous.

Israeli kids know that one day, when they grow up, they will have to go to the army and, perhaps, will have to fight Palestinians. When my brother was born (and he's eighteen now – he will start his military service in a few weeks) my mother hoped that he would not have to go to the army. But he has to, and he will, and I dread thinking where he will be sent after his basic training.

Boys like my brother are a legitimate target for you – but what choice do they have? Military service is compulsory, and they have to go to the units and places where they are sent. I, too, did my military service, and I was even an officer. I didn't serve in the Palestinian Territories, but many of my friends did, some of them in combat units. And even if they didn't like fighting, they had to justify it to themselves by developing a negative image of the Palestinians they were fighting against. How else would they be able to fight them?

Oh, Shireen. So many things have changed in the way I see things over the past few months, since I met you, and because I met you.

Maybe it's a cliché and perhaps it's obvious, but if both sides could educate their children to respect each other and to grow up as good neighbours, then there is a chance that those children who fear each other today could be good friends in the future.

One thing is certain – I would like us to make sure that our children remain friends, no matter what else goes on around us. We must find a way to get them together again in the near future, so that they develop that friendship. This is something I think of often.

Yours,
Daniela

★   ★   ★

November 29th, 2008
Ramallah

Dear Daniela,

Many things have changed in me since we met. Is it possible that so many things have changed in my mind, just because I met you? Imagine what could happen if there were many cases like ours. It would bring us closer to finding a solution.

It's so easy and, at the same time, so difficult. When I look around me, I see things only getting more complicated. It is difficult for me to admit, but my people only complicate things even more. Those who got used to fighting their whole life are now fighting each other. There is no excuse for what is happening here – why do we have to fight among ourselves? People can have different opinions politically, but we are all part of the same extended family. We are all neighbours, and even friends. In the same family you can find different political affiliations, and this is entirely normal.

I always thought of my people as rich in democratic culture. We always talked with each other, argued, debated.

We could tell jokes about one another. We always had the right to elect and to be elected. And I am certain that what is passing over us now is a black cloud which will disappear soon, *inshallah*.

I really find it hard to write this, but our internal wars don't bring us any gains. The only people who profit from them are you, Israelis. There is a proverb that says "divide and conquer" – we mustn't forget it and we need to understand that if we don't solve our own internal problems, we won't achieve anything. If we go on this way, we are the only losers.

I have no idea why I am writing this to you; this is a message for my people. I am finding it hard to concentrate and I think this letter is coming out a little vague. So perhaps I will now change the subject.

My little boy, Saif, has started talking, and is now making all sorts of demands. It's really funny – I think he started talking just so he could make all these demands! And my daughter Ghazal has started dressing herself up. She wants to wear jewellery – necklaces, earrings . . . and she is only six years old! God knows what will happen in a few years. Now I understand why my mother wanted to know each and every detail about my day when I was growing up.

I will end here, because my favourite television series is starting in a few minutes. You are more important, of course, but still, I've got to go . . .

Yours,
Shireen

* * *

CROSSING QALANDIYA

December 6th, 2008
Tel Aviv

Hello Shireen,

Today I thought of something I really want to share with you. It is something that had great influence on me when it happened, but I had sort of forgotten about it until just now.

A couple of years ago, when I was in the UK for a summer writing course, I met a very inspiring man. His name was Roy York, and he was a tutor in the Writing for Radio course I was taking at the time. We started chatting over coffee during the break, and when I told him I was Israeli, somehow we ended up talking about the army. He told me he was a soldier in the British Army in Palestine during the British Mandate. It was not easy for him to talk about those times, but here is what he told me:

When he was nineteen and serving in the British Army – he was a private, I think – he was sent to Palestine. His memories from his days there are very mixed, especially regarding the Jews. And why? Because the British soldiers knew that the Arabs wouldn't hurt them, but they had to be wary of the Jews.

He wasn't far from the King David Hotel[4] on July 22nd, 1946, when the *Etzel* resistance movement hid a bomb in the hotel basement – a bomb that killed nearly a hundred people and wounded dozens of others – among them some

---

4 The King David Hotel was the headquarters of the British Military in Jerusalem.

71

of his friends. He was also in a unit from which two soldiers were abducted by Jewish resistance members – or terrorists, even though I dread the word – and they killed them and hung their booby-trapped bodies on a tree. He was sent, with several others, to get the bodies, and he watched his commander blown up as he tried to take the bodies off the tree. I can't begin to imagine what other horrible memories he has from those days.

We keep in touch until this day, and he even sent me a copy of a BBC programme on the King David Hotel bombing. I must admit I am not particularly proud of these things – especially as some of the commanders and soldiers in this resistance movement later became our leaders.

Actually, I feel a chill going down my spine as I write these lines, because these are things I sort of knew about, but never really paid attention to. They are terrible events, and I don't like to think that my people had a part in them. But still, I feel that there is something a little more legitimate in fighting against soldiers than in random acts against civilians. When a bus explodes and passengers are killed and wounded, or a suicide bomber blows themselves up in a shopping mall, or even when a missile is launched without knowing exactly where it will hit – these are all inhumane actions. These are actions that cannot be justified by any amount of frustration and any strength of desire for independence.

Yours,
Daniela

* * *

December 11th, 2008
Ramallah

My friend,

How are you and how is your family? We are well, thank
God. The *Eid el Adha*, the festival of sacrifice, is taking place
this week, and I would like to tell you a bit more about it.

It is celebrated two months and ten days after *Eid el Fiter*,
and it corresponds with the end of the pilgrimage to Mecca, the
Hajj. Maybe I should start by telling you more about the *Hajj*.

The *Hajj* is a holy duty for every Muslim, a duty which
they must perform at least once in their lifetime. Every
Muslim has to pay for the pilgrimage themselves – it cannot
be done with someone else's money, or with money that is
borrowed. If you have children the duty of their education
and marriage takes precedence over the duty of the *Hajj*,
because they are both important ways of becoming closer to
God. You get bonus points for both, but as soon as a Muslim
can afford to pay the pilgrimage expenses, it is time.

When the pilgrim reaches Mecca and Medina in Saudi
Arabia, the first ceremony they perform is called *'waqfat
arafat'* – or 'standing on the mountain'.

It is the same mountain that the Prophet Muhammad
stood on when he performed his own pilgrimage, and where
he gave his last word to Muslims. According to the Holy
Koran, it is also the same mountain where the Prophet
Ibrahim was about to sacrifice his son, Ismail.

Each and every pilgrim has to climb up the mountain,
and when they come down they can start the ceremonies.
The first ceremony after descending the mountain is the

ahram – men cut their hair and wear white, seamless cloths, and women wear clothes (preferably white) which cover their entire bodies, except their faces and hands. During this period it is forbidden to engage in any unholy behaviour such as gossip, lying or feelings of hatred, because you need to be pure on both the inside and outside.

Sexual relations are forbidden during the time of the pilgrimage and, when it ends, the pilgrim has been cleansed of all their sins. All pilgrims end the *Hajj* wishing they could do it again, and when they come down the mountain, they celebrate the *Eid el Adha*. In Arabic, the word *adha* means sacrifice – therefore, the 'festival of sacrifice'.

However, I am sure you know that story – God provided a ram for the sacrifice once Ibrahim demonstrated his willingness to follow his commands[5].

After the sacrifice, a third of the meat goes to the poor, another third to family and friends, and the final third to the person who sacrificed the sheep. This holiday, too, involves the joy of wearing new clothes, getting holiday money and presents and, of course, eating sweets. So, as you can imagine, I am on a diet again. This celebration costs dearly, too, especially for the men!

What about you, my friend? Are you celebrating anything special these days? The New Year is approaching fast, so maybe my next letter will reach you in 2009!

---

5 It is well known to Muslims, Christians and Jews that Abraham was ordered to sacrifice his son and was willing to do so, but at the last minute God gave him a sheep to sacrifice instead of his cherished progeny. However, Jews and Christians say that the sacrificed was Isaac – "Abraham's only son", whereas according to the Islamic tradition it was Ishmael.

Before I finish, I would like you to know that I agree with what you wrote in your last letter. Of course violence is negative – but we did not invent this kind of action. Perhaps we even learned some of it from you, Israelis . . .?

Until next year,
Shireen

* * *

December 24th, 2008
Tel Aviv

Hello Shireen,

Thank you for your fascinating letter, which only reached me yesterday. Now, I think my last few letters have been very political, so this time I want to write something that will brighten your day a little.

Just as well, because this week we are celebrating *Hanukah*, the holiday of light. I am not sure why, but this is my favourite festival – maybe because it involves lighting candles and eating doughnuts and potato *latkes*!

You asked me a while ago if I, too, gain weight during the holidays. Well, during *Hanukah* I always do, because I can't resist the delicious jam-filled doughnuts (or sometimes they are filled with chocolate, condensed milk and all sorts of culinary inventions from the last few years . . . but when I was a child, there were only simple, jam-filled doughnuts, and they were the best!) which are extremely rich – even more so than your *maamul*s.

During *Hanukah* (which lasts eight days) we also light a new candle every evening, starting with one on the eve of the holiday, and ending with eight candles on the last day.

And all this why?

Because nearly 2200 years ago, in the time of the Second Temple, Antiochus the Greek ruled over the land of Israel and wanted to convert all the Jews. The Greeks damaged the Temple and destroyed all the Jewish holy artefacts inside (apparently I can't avoid including some mention of conflict in my letter!). When the Jews entered the temple to survey the damage, they found one small can of oil for a holy candle-holder which was supposed to burn with an eternal fire. This small can would normally have lasted no more than a day, but the miracle of *Hanukah* is that it supposedly lasted for eight days, giving them time to press more oil for the lamp.

So, this is why we light candles for eight days and eat foods fried in oil . . . whether it is a good reason or an excuse to eat fattening foods I cannot say, but one thing is certain – these holiday specialities are absolutely delicious. Also, *Hanukah* is not a particularly religious holiday, and this makes me enjoy it even more. I have nothing against religion (especially Judaism, of course) but I do have a lot against those who use religion as a means to force their beliefs on others, and don't let others live as they see fit.

I hope I am not offending you by making comments critical of religion. I was actually surprised to learn that you are a practising Muslim, because I used to think that practising Muslims were all very radical. You certainly don't look radical to me! I am sure there are many beautiful aspects to all religions, and it is just sad that people tarnish religion by committing horrendous acts in the name of it – acts that no God would approve of.

Yours,
Daniela

P.S. I was really interested to read about the *Hajj*, but I still don't understand why they have to sacrifice a sheep.

★   ★   ★

January 2nd, 2009
Ramallah

Dear Daniela,

I am writing to you despite the fact that I feel exhausted. I have hardly slept over the last few nights. I constantly watch the news on television, and it makes me sad. It's so difficult to watch civilians, children, being hurt. Being killed in Gaza. It's just awful. Only God can help us, my dear Daniela, to get out of this situation. It is time that our children had a normal life, without this constant fear in their eyes.

You are right about what you wrote in your last letter about religion. I consider myself to be a religious Muslim, though perhaps it is hard to tell from looking at me. It doesn't always show on the outside. I would like to tell you a little more about my religion, about Islam.

The most important things in our religion as I see it are human behaviour and moral values. My religion stresses their importance, and so do I. I respect all my duties towards God and towards society: I don't lie, I don't cheat and I never say one thing to a person's face and another behind their back.

77

The only thing I do not do is cover my head – and I would do that, too, if it were important to my husband for reasons of modesty.

Modesty is a must in our religion, but it doesn't mean that if I don't cover my head I am not considered a religious Muslim. In the same way, it does not mean that when a woman does cover her head, she is an extremist. She is merely being modest.

As to other religions, I respect all of them. I have always had friends from other faiths, and religion has nothing to do with the choice of my friends. I choose my friends according to their character and their moral values.

I also teach my children that there are big differences between places and people, and that they should accept things as they are. It is inconceivable that they not be able to accept that there are cultural differences. Everyone deserves a choice, and if you respect other people's choices, they will respect yours. I try to explain these things to my kids in a simple way, and this is not unusual. All of my family and friends see things in a similar way.

I would really like to change your perception of us, the negative image that we have in the eyes of your people and in the eyes of the world. Being a Muslim does not mean being an extremist. The real Muslims are those who have high moral values, and many of my people do. What we need to work on is our image and the way we voice our opinions.

Yes, we really are good people who want to live in a peaceful and civilised manner. This is the way of life that we would have chosen for ourselves. That we do choose for ourselves.

I am getting so carried away that I nearly forgot to congratulate you on the New Year – I hope it will be one full of peace and love. Normally we would have celebrated New Year's Eve with close friends and family, but this year we just stayed at home with some friends. They came to our house not to celebrate, but to watch the news from Gaza together.

My wish for this New Year, which has started in such an awful way, is that it will end with two states living side by side in peace.

Yours,
Shireen

January 6th, 2009
Ramallah

Dear Daniela,

I am really feeling down today, which is why I am writing to you despite having written only a few days ago.

Today I met a friend who had made a New Year's resolution to try and work outside Palestine. She is looking for work in Europe, and she attempted to fill out some application forms online. She asked for my help, as my English is better than hers, so we sat down together and started filling out the forms for a position with an international company.

But very quickly we got stuck on one rather essential detail: country of citizenship. There was a list of options and we needed to select the right country. But, of course, Palestine was not on that list. There was no way to add on the name of a country, and she did not want to put Israel, or even Jordan, as her country of citizenship. What choice did she have? She decided not to send in the form.

Is this fair, I ask you? We've been around for centuries, and everyone knows we're here. So why can't we have our own country, like everyone else in the world? I don't have words to describe my feelings to you, my friend. I feel such heartache; it really brings me down.

But of course, I don't give up. If I allow myself to feel defeated, I will only lose. I will never renounce my right for my own state, and I don't want my kids to have the same feeling I have – of being stateless.

So please help me, my friend. We must find a way for our people to stop fighting. Life is too short to be lived like this. After all, we all want to live in peace and we all want what is best for our children.

So why is it so difficult to get it?

Shireen

★   ★   ★

January 14th, 2009
Tel Aviv

Dear Shireen,

Imagine my surprise and delight in finding two letters from you in my mailbox on the same day. I have thought of you often over the past few days because of what is happening in Gaza, and of course I am sad and outraged about civilians getting hurt and killed – on both sides. And most of all, it pains me to see children suffer. It really is time that our children stop living in fear, especially in fear of one another. They should be able to live carefree, like other children in the world.

What else can I say, except that I hope that your people can understand that the actions of Hamas are not serving your interests, and that Israel is now fighting Hamas, and not the Palestinian people as a whole. And what choice do we have?

No one here is happy to see Palestinian civilians suffering, but despite the fact that there are many Israelis who don't agree the war in Gaza is absolutely necessary, everyone agrees that Hamas rockets hitting Israeli towns must be stopped.

Despite everything that is going on, I wish you and your family a Happy New Year. Actually, I am surprised you are marking the Gregorian New Year – I didn't know Muslims celebrated it!

Here there are some who celebrate it and some who don't. Everyone celebrates the Jewish New Year in September, but the civil New Year serves mostly as an excuse to go out and party or invite people over.

Before we had kids, we used to go to parties, but over the past five years or so we've become less adventurous. In any case, this year nobody felt like partying, because of the war in southern Israel and Gaza. Still, we went for a walk on the promenade in Tel Aviv and ate in a beach-front restaurant with some friends. Then we invited everyone back to our place and, after we put our kids to bed, we had some wine and watched the news. And of course, when we discussed politics and the situation in general I told them about our friendship.

Just so you know, they were extremely curious about our exchange, and they said they'd like to take part in it, too – that they'd like to prepare a list of questions for you, because they really want to know you – and your people – better. Despite some initial cynical comments (such as, 'that's great, Daniela, you're contributing to the Peace Process') they were very moved when I told them some of the things I had learned from you. And they, like most Israelis, would like to live with you side by side, in peace. So beware – from now on you might not only get questions from me, but from my friends, too!

I do agree that you need to have your own state; the sooner the better. And this is not only for your sake, but for ours, too. For your sake, because you deserve to be able to control your own destiny (but when you do have your own state, you may see that it isn't so easy – we are a good example), and for our sake because I really think there is no justification for the continued occupation. I have found myself going through a process over the past few months, a sort of understanding that took me from believing that 'everything is your fault' through 'perhaps it is a little bit our fault, too' all the way to the conclusion that we actually share the blame – equally. Without undermining your responsibility for the situation, I would like to be able to be honest enough with myself and with you and to address our own responsibly, which definitely exists.

It is true that it is perhaps easier to be in a position of power, but I really think that this position of power is now ruining us. It separates my people and causes our morals to decline. We always took pride in being a moral people. You may laugh, but yes, I believed in it, too, until very recently. But we are raising generations of children, youths and adults who develop the mentality of 'occupiers'.

So yes, it is unfair that you and your friend don't have a 'country of citizenship' to fill out in the job application form. And I do hope that this coming year will be a good one for you – and for us. A year of independence and self determination for you, but not at the cost of our security. I'd like you to be able to live next to us and with us – if not as friends, at least as good neighbours.

I've already told you that I've spoken to many friends and relatives about our correspondence. There were very few negative reactions – most people were thrilled to hear about it. They were glad to know that such a friendship can exist. I hope that later this year we will be able to sit together, in Tel Aviv or in Ramallah, and have coffee again and watch our children play – without fearing each other. How do you say in Arabic – *inshallah*?

Yours,
Daniela

★   ★   ★

January 20th, 2009
Ramallah

Dear Daniela,

I was very happy to receive your last letter, but I feel I must put something straight before I get into other things. You wrote that Israel is now fighting Hamas and not the Palestinian people as a whole. Just to tell you, my dear, that Hamas *are* the Palestinian people and they are part of our family. In many Palestinian families you will find some brothers who support Hamas and others who support Fatah. This is our reality. From my point of view, targeting Hamas is not the solution – you are just making things more complicated.

83

I am hoping that writing to you will help alleviate some of the frustration I am feeling right now. I've been under a lot of pressure today, over a family matter involving my younger sister. You may imagine it is a little girl I am talking about, but no – she is twenty-four years old.

The whole thing started with her planning a holiday in Europe – the first in her life. She's been saving money for this trip for a very long time. But the problems started when she asked for her first-ever tourist visa to Europe. I would never have thought that one visa application could cause so much stress and so many problems over just two months.

She applied for the visa over eight weeks ago, but received it only four days ago, less than forty-eight hours before her flight. Following orders from the consulate, she had paid for and bought her ticket a long time in advance.

She's been under terrible stress over the past few weeks – would she or wouldn't she get the visa? Each time they asked for another piece of paper, and each time she sent it in, they remembered that they needed one more thing.

I've applied for tourist visas to Europe in the past, and I've always got them within a couple of weeks, which is very reasonable. And even if my sister had received a negative response within two weeks, we would have thought this understandable. But why cause someone so much grief for no reason?

Apparently, it all came down to one heartless employee in the consulate in Jerusalem. I write this with all due respect, of course. But when my sister finally called and asked to speak to the consul's assistant – having found out his name from some friends of friends – the same heartless employee completed the procedures that same day. And my sister didn't even get to speak to the consul's assistant – he was out! Just mentioning his name was enough.

I am sure you cannot imagine how difficult it is to get so much as a piece of paper from Nablus (where my sister still lives, in my parents' home) to Jerusalem. After all, it isn't like we can take the documents in personally. Each and every piece of paper has to be sent through a courier service, so my sister ended up paying over one thousand shekels to Aramex over eight weeks.

Anyway, this part was done. My sister got her visa, boarded the plane in Amman and landed in Paris. Then my brother – who lives in Sweden – called out of the blue to ask me if our little sister had arrived safely. I said she had, and he started asking questions, questions and more questions: Who did she go with? Why did she go? Where will she sleep? And on and on . . .

Of course I knew who she went with and where she was staying – with friends! But in our culture people have a different attitude towards these things. It isn't easy for a girl to travel on her own; the community doesn't approve. Some do, but most people perceive it in a negative way.

When he couldn't get the answers he wanted from me, my brother called my sister's mobile and started questioning *her*. After everything she had gone through to get her visa, he set about ruining her trip.

I am not saying he intended this – but this is what happened. And what else can he do? He grew up in a community that thinks this way. It is problematic because, according to Islam, women cannot travel on their own, but must be accompanied by a male relative, such as a husband, father, brother or uncle.

Saying that, a woman can travel in a group with other women – if her family trusts these women. Islam does not say that women should not travel and have a good time, but that they should do it in reliable and respectable company.

My poor sister. My heart goes out to her, and I am stuck in the middle between her and my brother. I just got another angry call, because he thinks our sister is not mature enough to be taking this trip on her own. He says he lives in Europe and he knows from experience that it's a very bad idea for a young girl to hang around on her own. He wants her to come to his place in Sweden and spend her holiday there . . . she, of course, wants to stay with her friends.

Daniela, my head hurts from the arguments I've had with him, and with her, too. But, fingers crossed, I think that following our last conversation he was finally convinced that he should leave her alone.

I am sorry to burden you with all of this – I haven't even asked how you are doing. So how are you, and how are your husband and kids?

Yours,
Shireen

★   ★   ★

January 30th, 2009
Tel Aviv

Hello Shireen,

My heart really goes out to your sister. Twenty-four years old . . . wow. Here, no one would blink if a girl her age wanted to go on her own to Europe. Of course, parents are always concerned, that is natural. But if young people here go to Europe, the parents are actually happy. Most young Israelis go to more exotic places like Thailand and India, where it is perhaps more risky to travel than in Europe: muggings, accidents, drugs, and who knows what else.

Of course, religious families are different. I guess a religious young woman wouldn't travel on her own, for reasons similar to those you've described. But I grew up in a very secular society, and it seems entirely normal to me that a twenty-four year old woman would want to travel on her own and meet up with friends – female or male.

If your sister is intelligent and responsible – which I am sure she is – then she should take responsibility over her life and her actions, isn't it so? I feel that in your heart you agree, which is why you've intervened in her favour. But it must be very difficult to live with this dilemma; religion on the one hand and reality on the other.

I am also sure there are good reasons why religion indicates that women shouldn't travel alone – after all, two thousand years ago, what woman in her right mind would think of hopping on a camel and going for a stroll in the desert unaccompanied . . .?

But some things have changed since then, and even if there is still evil in the world, and there are some evil people out there, at least there are social institutions that are designed to keep law and order.

I must confess that at the age of twenty-two, I backpacked on my own around South Africa. I wasn't

alone, but went with a travelling companion, also from
Israel. He was a guy I met through a travel-equipment
shop that also had a notice board for people looking for
someone to travel with. We arranged to meet in
Johannesburg and hired a car together. We then drove
around and slept at youth-hostels, where there were
separate rooms for men and women. But after a few days
I realised that this guy was really not my type of person –
not from a romantic point of view (there was never
any question of that) – I just didn't enjoy travelling
with him.

I decided to continue the trip on my own. I had a
distant, elderly relative, whom I'd never met before, in
Durban, so I took the bus and spent a few nice days with
her. She was an impressive woman. She lived on her own
in a lovely apartment not far from the beach, and told me
many interesting stories about her youth and life in South
Africa. Thanks to her, I felt very much at home. Then I
found new people to travel with – this time from New
Zealand – and we had much more in common than I'd had
with the Israeli guy. I spent the rest of the trip with them,
and it was a life-changing experience because I was on my
own and made my own decisions. I took responsibility for
my actions, for better or worse.

I didn't mention that I went on this trip after splitting
up with a boyfriend I had really loved, so it was partly a
way of helping me get over him and getting rid of the
sadness and sorrow I felt back then.

You know, I actually think that it is much easier for a
woman travelling on her own to meet people and make
new friends, because lots of people are keen to help her . . .

but don't tell your brother this. He'll only say that Israelis set a bad example, and that I am a bad influence on you!

So yes, we have many things in common, but this is one area where our societies seem to differ. But that is what makes our exchange so interesting.

In any case, I hope your sister enjoys her trip and doesn't take the harsh criticism to heart. This experience will only make her stronger and broaden her horizons. But, of course, that doesn't mean that she shouldn't be careful and look after herself. After all, a girl travelling on her own . . .

Love,
Daniela

P.S. I honestly didn't realise that you couldn't come to Jerusalem, not even for a short visit or, as in your sister's case, to ask for a visa.

★   ★   ★

February 6th, 2009
Ramallah

Hello Daniela,

The fact that we live in the same part of the world means we have a lot in common: the foods we eat, the drinks we drink, the weather we are used to . . . I just remembered a trip I once took with my husband, who helped organise a youth peace conference in Greece. We travelled with the other Palestinian organisers, but once there we met with young people from all over the world – including Israel.

And the funny thing was that we ended up spending a lot of time with the Israeli youths. We spoke, we argued and, when it was time to eat, we inevitably met by the same dishes at the buffet. We chose the same food, and were the only two delegations who didn't touch the pork dishes!

So if we can agree on the important issue of food, why can't we agree on a few other things?

You wrote that you are letting some of your family and friends know about our exchange. I've started doing the same thing. I am convinced that when people hear about what we are doing, they go and tell other people. Who knows, maybe one day we'll have played a small part in facilitating the understanding and exchange between our peoples. Or do you think this is only a dream?

Philosophising aside – again, I have forgotten to ask how you are doing. So, how are you and yours? My big news is that one of my girl friends gave birth to a baby girl a few days ago. I love visiting newborns in the hospital; I am enchanted by the first few days in a baby's life.

This friend is also a work colleague, and we've been through a lot together – good and bad. So I've collected money from everyone at our office to buy a present for her, so she can choose something she really wants.

Well, I have to end here because my son Saif just woke up. I'd like to get him back in bed straight away before he decides he isn't tired . . .

Yours,
Shireen

P.S. Just before sending this letter, I remembered that you asked me a while ago why we sacrifice a lamb in the *Hajj*, and I'm not sure I answered your question. The answer is that the prophet Ibrahim sacrificed a lamb in the place of his son, Ishmael. I think this story is one more thing we have in common?

The sheep is sacrificed to commemorate the willingness of the Prophet Ibrahim to sacrifice his son as an act of obedience to God.

★　★　★

February 16th, 2009
Tel Aviv

Hello Shireen,

How are you and how are things? All well, I hope.

I was very amused by the P.S. in your last letter. Of course I know the story of Abraham . . . from our bible classes at school. But our version is slightly different. It was Isaac who was about to be sacrificed by Abraham, and not Ishmael. Finally, we have discovered the point when things started to go wrong!

But joking aside, I am amazed to discover how much we have in common. And this makes our conflict even less comprehensible to me. How did two such similar peoples reach such a situation of misunderstanding, of mutual hatred? If only everyone could know the things we've been discovering over the past few months . . .

Please congratulate your friend on my behalf – is this her first baby? If so, very soon she will find out the truth behind her baby's adorable little face, and how much this small creature is about to change her life!

Unlike you, I don't like visiting newborns in hospital. I remember how I felt in the first few days after birth, and how I didn't want to see anyone other than my husband and my son for the first week or so.

I think that as cute as babies are, I prefer them walking and talking. Then at least I can understand what the howling is all about and can ask them to play on their own for a few minutes and give me a break!

We have the same custom of collecting money at work for a joint present for special occasions and births. I think everyone in the world does this, but maybe I'm wrong. If a baby boy is born, there is the circumcision ceremony on the eighth day. If it's a girl, sometimes we also have a small gathering or celebration, just to mark the occasion. Of course, nothing is being chopped off then.

This celebration is usually the first opportunity for everyone to see the newborn baby, but I must say that I object to the custom where the male circumcision is performed in front of everyone by a rabbi. The baby suffers while everyone around him celebrates and stuffs their faces with food. I find it horrific. We did circumcise our two boys, but at the doctor's office, quietly and under medical supervision. Then, when the baby feels better, everyone can celebrate. This is what we've done, anyway.

I know that you circumcise your boys, too, but I think it isn't always on the eighth day, like us. Or is it?

I will stop here because I have to call a taxi to take me to the garage, where our car is being repaired. I hope I can find a reliable driver who will come quickly, because I have to go and pick up the kids from kindergarten at four o'clock.

Yours,
Daniela

★   ★   ★

February 23rd, 2009
Ramallah

Hi Daniela,

My kids have gone to bed, and I'm finally sitting down to write to you, with a cup of coffee by my side. I enjoy writing these letters – it is so different from emails. It feels much more creative and personal, more magical and warm. And we can re-read the letters, and see each other's handwriting. I am glad you seem to feel the same.

Since you mentioned in your last letter that you were looking for a reliable taxi driver (I hope your car is fixed by now), I thought this might be a good opportunity to tell you about one of those experiences in my life which seemed difficult at the time, but now brings back happy memories. It has to do with a taxi driver called Bilaal. I think I've mentioned his name in the past, but now I'd like to tell you the whole story.

This is a man who accompanied me through each and every stage of my adult life, and I will never forget the first day I got into his taxi. It was a normal day, early in the morning, and I was making my way from Nablus to my day job in Ramallah as usual.

And like most mornings, I was with a group of seven friends, including one of my cousins. We prepared to cross the Hawara check-point (between Nablus and Ramallah) on foot, as we did every day.

After crossing the check-point, we always continued further down the road, to a place where taxis wait to take people onwards to Ramallah. We took the first one available – all seven of us together.

We started driving towards Ramallah, and we couldn't help noticing that the driver was particularly friendly. And he wasn't just friendly, but also quick and efficient -what we call in Arabic *'falawii'* – someone who knows how to get out of any situation. When we reached Ramallah, we asked him if he'd meet us every morning at the Hawara check-point, and he agreed. And this is how the story of Bilaal started.

Every weekday, for over a year, we confronted the difficult drive from Nablus to Ramallah and back together. We learned to appreciate Bilaal, his intelligence and his intuition. He knew all the smallest roads and dirt tracks, and we were always the first to get where we were going.

And these weren't just ordinary roads – he'd always take us via the scenic route, through small tracks and tiny villages. He turned our excruciating daily commute into something that was almost enjoyable. Of course, it was still an exhausting routine, but it is thanks to him that I know my country so well.

Even in the most difficult moments, I was able to smile and say to my travel-mates, 'Don't worry. It may take us three hours to get to work, but at least we are broadening our horizons and getting lessons in the geography of Palestine!' We used to call the rides with Bilaal the 'get to know your country' course.

When I met my dear husband, and he came to ask my family's permission to marry me, he came with Bilaal. Then, when he arrived with his family to sign the marriage agreement, they, too, took that trip with Bilaal.

And I didn't think twice about whom to ask for a ride on my wedding day – but I have already told you about that day and don't want to repeat the tale. And even after I was married, my relationship with Bilaal continued. It was he who took me to my parents' house with my two-week-old daughter, so she could meet her grandparents for the first time. And I made the same trip with him again after the birth of my second child, Saif, three years later.

Of course, every time someone is looking for a reliable taxi driver, I recommend Bilaal. And, if one day you'd like to come and visit me, you won't be able to drive to Ramallah with your Israeli licence plates, so I shall send Bilaal to collect you.

So you see, even if there are moments in life that seem difficult or negative, in the long run they can become pleasant memories, in part. Sometimes I miss those difficult days . . . not the daily crossing of check-points and road-blocks, Daniela, but the life I lived as a young woman, before I was married with all these responsibilities.

After the story of Bilaal it is difficult to write about other things. So I will end here.

Yours,
Shireen

$\star$ $\star$ $\star$

Dear Shireen,

I love your story about Bilaal. You can already let him know that when I come to visit you one day, I will definitely come with him. I know that some years ago it was still possible to drive to Ramallah with Israeli licence plates, but I think this is no longer the case. I hope it will change soon.

I've told you that some of my friends and family members know about our exchange, and I have already threatened you with the long list of questions they are preparing. Of course, I don't expect you to answer all these questions right away, but I'd like to ask you a few of them – especially as I know the list is growing rapidly! So here is what they would like to know about you so far:

My younger brother's girlfriend wants to know what young women can and can't do in your society. What happens if a girl meets a man she likes – can she date him? What kind of relationship can they have?

My brother's question is related to polygamy. Is it true that a man can marry more than one woman (I think he likes the idea . . .)? If so, how do his wives feel about it? (This one is actually my own question!)

My friend Yael is interested in the type of music young people listen to. Is it mainly Arab, or do they listen to western music, too?

CROSSING QALANDIYA

My friend Alon wants to know about the *nakbah*, and I second his question. When we celebrate our Independence Day, you mark your *nakbah*, your disaster. Why is that? Why is it such a disaster that we have our own state? After all, the Palestinian Authority now recognises the State of Israel.

Maybe I should stop here and let you answer whatever you'd like to answer. And feel free to send me questions back. I think that if we can expand our correspondence to include more people who are interested in one another, perhaps something good will come out of it.

You know, when I was ten or twelve, many of my friends and I had pen-pals from all over the world. We learned about the lives of young people from many different countries, because it was important to us to know how people lived in other cultures and other places, like Europe, Australia, Africa and Japan. But what about you, our neighbours? I think we simply forgot you existed . . . perhaps conveniently so.

Yours,
Daniela

* * *

March 9th, 2009
Ramallah

Hi Daniela,

There are so many things that we have in common, yet so many things that are different, and it is only natural. Even in the same family, each child is different.

97

I am writing to you only now, my dear, and it is late – after midnight. It's the only time I have to myself, after I have finished all my other duties: work, house, kids and husband. I really don't have much energy after all this, but here I am, writing to you, my Israeli friend. So what will I write about today?

You've asked in one of your previous letters about circumcision. We do circumcise our boys, and we call it *'tuhur'*, meaning purification, since we believe the circumcision purifies the child. However, there is no specific time or date for the procedure to take place, although they recommend you do it as early as possible. Most people circumcise their sons about two weeks after birth.

The man who performs the circumcision is called *'mutahar'* – the purifier. He usually comes to the home of the baby about to be circumcised, but these days more and more people perform the procedure at a hospital. This is what we did with our son, and the same doctor who delivered him also circumcised him – a few days later.

After the circumcision we give everyone sweets, and all the relatives – grandparents, brothers, sisters, uncles and aunts – come home in the evening to celebrate. We don't celebrate during the circumcision, but a few hours later, when the baby is much calmer.

I always tell my husband that this is the only real suffering that men go through during their lifetime and, fortunately for them, it is done when they are very young. This way they forget the pain very quickly. But for us, women, there is much more suffering, much later in life.

And, as I have mentioned suffering, since my little boy was born I have awful back aches. I am not sure why this is, but I had an epidural shot right before the birth, and although the doctor says there is no connection, I believe there is. Do women usually ask for an epidural when giving birth in Israel? I know that in Europe most do. But here only a fraction of women ask for one; most give birth naturally. This is now reminding me of the pain of the first birth – they say that pain is different from those that follow, because you don't know what to expect and you've never experienced that kind of agony before.

When I was pregnant with Ghazal and started having contractions, there was a curfew imposed by the Israeli army. But we didn't think much – we just got in the car and drove to the hospital. Thank God we arrived there without anyone stopping us; we took a real risk. Soldiers often shoot at vehicles driving during a curfew, and there are many women (and men) who have died this way.

Anyway, I only stayed in hospital one night, because it was a normal birth, and left the next day. The curfew was still on, and this time we were stopped by a soldier.

"Why are you driving during a curfew?" he asked, and my husband told him I had just given birth and showed him the baby and the birth certificate. Fortunately the birth certificate was in both Arabic and English, so he read it and let us go.

Before the birth, when I asked my husband if he would come into the delivery room with me, he said "No way, I won't be able to face that". But when the moment came, he stayed with me during the whole birth and even cut the umbilical cord himself. My mother, who came from Nablus especially to be with me during the birth, didn't even get to come in, because only one person was allowed in at any time. That one person was my husband, and of course he did the same again the second time around. He says that these moments are among the happiest in his life.

What about you? Did your husband attend the births of your children?

Daniela, I really can't take these back aches anymore. I think I'll go and see a doctor tomorrow. And I will go to bed now – it is already one o'clock and I have to get up in a few short hours, to start another day.

Kisses,
Shireen

★   ★   ★

March 16th, 2009
Tel Aviv

Shireen *Shalom,*

The most appropriate opening for my letter would be to quote the so called 'Curse of Eve' from the book of Genesis in the Old Testament: "In pain you shall bring forth children" or something similar . . . wasn't this Eve's punishment when she was sent away from paradise? I think that up to this point in history we still see eye to eye.

It was very interesting reading about your experiences of giving birth. After all, these are the true existential things that we do share, regardless of politics, geography or religion.

It shows that at the end of the day, we are all just human beings, coming from the same place and probably going to the same place, too. So why do we have to fight so much along the way?

When I gave birth to my two boys, my husband was also present. He, too, was not sure he'd be able to face it at first. What do you think of that? We are the ones giving birth and dealing with the pain, and they are the ones who cannot face it. Nice.

But I was more afraid of the epidural needle than of the pain of giving birth (did you actually see that monstrosity before they stuck it through your back?) and so gratefully declined the offer.

So I gave birth without epidural both times, and I think more and more women here are now opting for a natural birth. But yes, most women do ask for it because they probably think they won't be able to take the pain, or perhaps it is because the doctors convince them that the suffering is not worth it. I disagree.

I think that just as all animals give birth without pain control, so can humans. And I actually saw it as a challenge to face something natural, and that comes from a divine and uplifting place inside us.

I think that if you don't feel any pain during birth, you miss out on part of the experience – but this is just my opinion, of course. Each and every woman should have and make her own choice.

Of course the births were painful, but before my second birth I went through training for, you'll never guess, self hypnosis. Bear with me here, before you decide that I am completely nuts. The course was given by an American woman, and it was really wonderful. Let me tell you more.

The method is based on the belief that if you are afraid and tense, then so are your muscles. When the muscles in your body contract involuntarily, so do the muscles of your uterus. But, if you are calm and relaxed, and your muscles are relaxed, your pain will decrease. And the way that you relax yourself and your muscles is what they call "self hypnosis", but it is really just a relaxation method, like meditation. It includes exercises that should be done every evening at bedtime, from the fourth or fifth month onwards, and then repeated during the birth itself. But by then you are so used to these breathing and relaxation exercises that they feel very natural.

And I have to tell you that it did work for me. I won't say that I didn't feel any pain during that second birth, but it was pain that could be controlled, and certainly less scary than that long epidural needle.

I'm not a doctor, but I wouldn't be surprised if your back aches are indeed related to the epidural. I heard from many girl friends who had it that they suffered the same problem later. I do hope you are feeling better – it's horrible having back pain, especially when you have to look after two kids *and* go to work every day.

By the way, maybe you could tell me a little more about your work? You told me when we met in Geneva that you work for the Palestinian Investment Promotion Agency in Ramallah, but I am very curious to know how you promote investments when the political situation is so tense. It can't be easy.

Yours,
Daniela

CROSSING QALANDIYA

*   *   *

March 21st, 2009
Ramallah

Daniela,

Today is Mother's Day, and the first day of spring. And, as always, I have mixed feelings. I feel joy and love, but also sadness. I don't know if I am 'for' or 'against' commemorating this day, because it is a celebration for some, but a day of great sadness for others – for all those women who've lost their children.

It was very interesting for me, too, to read about your birthing experience. You don't look like someone who is afraid of needles, but you are right to be scared of this one. It really does look terrible. I hesitated a lot before I decided to have the epidural, and when the anaesthetist came into the room, my husband was sitting next to me. He took one look at the bearded doctor, and asked: "So, are you from Hamas?"

It's important to mention that Saif was born just a few days after Hamas won the elections. The doctor said that no, he wasn't from Hamas and that the fact he had a beard did not mean anything of the kind.

Then he started fiddling with his instruments and I was shaking with fear – since I had been told that one small error on the anaesthetist's part could cause a lifetime of paralysis – when my husband started discussing politics, there and then. And, believe it or not, the doctor joined in!

I asked them both to concentrate on me and the needle I was about to have stuck in my back, instead of on politics.

The doctor just laughed – he said that everything would be fine, and not to worry. Of course I worried.

Then came the actual birth and I was in so much pain. And suddenly I hear my husband start discussing politics with the obstetrician, too! With all admiration for the doctor, who is one of the best, I could not hold myself back. I shouted, 'Stop it, you two! Let me give birth in peace and then sort out your political issues!'

It didn't really help, but thank God, everything was ok. My son Saif is now two and a half, and everything is a distant memory. And if we ignore the pain, then it is actually quite an amusing memory.

In your last letter you asked me about my job. It's strange that I haven't discussed it more with you, because all my friends at work know about you and about our exchange. Seems that I forgot to tell you about them!

Like I told you in Geneva, I work for PIPA, the Palestinian Investment Promotion Agency in Ramallah. I am the Director for International Cooperation, and the work is very interesting, but of course, the political circumstances are not great. And, as a result, there aren't many investments coming in.

Our main objective is to encourage investments in Palestine, and especially foreign investment. How do you convince people to invest money in a place that is not politically stable? Good question.

But still, there are people who invest, and invest quite a lot. At the same time, since we are not drowning in work, our Director General decided that in order to maximise productivity it would be a good time to send us on various training courses, so we'll be ready when the time comes. Many of these training courses take place right here in Ramallah, but some take place abroad. Some of us have attended training programmes in Jordan, Italy, France and more.

I, for example, was sent to attend a course in Marseilles, on Strategic Marketing. And since I have mentioned this course, I must tell you an amusing related story.

On the first day we all walked the short distance from the hotel to the conference hall. I was nicely dressed, nicely made up, I had my hair done . . . in short, I looked good.

A man in his forties walked next to me, smiled and then suddenly asked:

"Where are you from? I'm from Israel."

"In that case, we are cousins," I said. "I'm from Palestine."

He looked baffled for a moment, but then said:

"I am sorry, I don't hear very well. Where are you from, Pakistan?"

"Not Pakistan. Palestine," I said. "We are neighbours."

He froze in his spot, and then mumbled, quite embarrassed:

"Very nice to meet you."

But he did then try to be friendly towards me during the rest of the conference, despite the fact that I was not particularly nice to him.

Daniela Norris and Shireen Anabtawi

Back to the subject of my work. When things improve, we'll be prepared to dedicate all our efforts to promoting our agency and foreign investments in Palestine. All my colleagues are more or less the same age, in their twenties and thirties, and even our Director General is young, in his early forties. It's a really nice working environment.

What about you? I know that you're a writer, but please tell me more about what you do.

I will end here, because on Mother's Day we always go to my mother-in-law's. As I am married, tradition is that most holidays are celebrated at my in-laws' (not everyone follows this rule, there are some exceptions), because it shows respect to my husband and his family.

Yours,
Shireen

★   ★   ★

March 28th, 2009
Tel Aviv

Hi Shireen,

I laughed so hard when I read your last letter – giving birth to a backdrop of political debate and avoiding Israelis who think you're Pakistani! I think we could write a great comedy about all the trouble we cause one another, and all the nonsense we believe. If only it weren't so painful.

The thing is, if we could find a way to laugh about it, despite the pain and the sorrow, perhaps there is a chance that people would start crawling out of these fortresses they've built for protection, on both sides of the conflict.

106

Maybe they'd start believing that we could treat each other more humanely and see things in a less absolute way. I am certain this will begin soon – I can feel it in the air.

Yes, it is strange that we haven't discussed our work more until now. As I told you in Geneva, I used to work for the Israeli Ministry of Foreign Affairs. I worked with them for seven years. Then something happened that made me reconsider things; in fact, a few things happened in parallel.

When I was about to finish my two-year posting to Lima, Peru, a young diplomat was assigned to replace me in my job as Second Secretary dealing with Cultural, Media and Political Affairs. His name was David. He was a very bright young man, who had been born in Argentina and immigrated with his family to Israel in his childhood. He spoke fluent Spanish, of course, which was great for the job, and he came for a working visit to Lima to sort out a place to live, a car and generally learn the ropes. It was to be his first posting.

I took him round to meet all my colleagues. He liked the apartment I lived in and took over the lease. He also bought my little green Golf from me, so he could drive himself around as soon as he got there. That's the way he was – he took life head on. He then went back to Israel because he had some exams to write and papers to hand in for his Masters degree at the Hebrew University in Jerusalem. After the last exams, he was to return to Lima so I could leave and join my then boyfriend, now husband, who had already had to leave Lima to start a new job.

David never made it back. He was killed while having lunch in the cafeteria of the Hebrew University after handing in his last paper for his Masters degree. It was one week before he was supposed to take over the assignment in Lima. Someone hid a bomb in a sports bag in the cafeteria and it exploded and killed nine people, injuring many others. They think it was one of the Arab employees who worked at the Hebrew University. Why, Shireen? I will never be able to understand this.

This young man did nothing wrong. He was kind, smart, funny, a humanist and a pacifist, excited about the challenges he was about to take on and the opportunities the life ahead of him had to offer. He was twenty-nine years old when he died.

He had left some clothes in my apartment in Lima – he went shopping on his visit, for suits, ties, nice things to wear to his new job – so I had to pack them all up and send them to his parents. I stayed on in Lima for a while, but then had to leave and join Jonathan, my future husband. We'd been apart for six months by then. One of the first things I did when back in Israel was visit David's parents – a charming elderly couple, who were left with very little else in life. David was not their only son, but he was their pride and joy. It was such a tragedy.

I then took a year off to complete an MBA in Paris, where Jonathan had a job at the time. That same year I married him, had our first son, and then my second the following year. I decided to leave the Ministry of Foreign Affairs because I wanted to distance myself from having to constantly deal with the tragic situation in our region; from being a mouth piece of the Israeli Government. Yes, I still want to serve the interests of my country. But I believe that I am serving them better by following my passion and writing – writing the truth as I see it. Writing from the point of view of an Israeli who can see the terrible suffering of both sides, and who feels for both.

I believe that the best thing for my country would be to have a peaceful co-existence with our neighbours, and since meeting you I am even more convinced of this. After all, we are very much alike, and have more in common than most people can imagine. It is the attitude that needs to change – on both sides. Then other things can start happening.

So now I write, and spend more time with my two young boys. I started publishing short stories and articles in international magazines, and it was my work for the Geneva Times that brought me there when we met.

Writing can be a lonesome affair, but I enjoy my days. I take my boys to kindergarten in the morning dressed in jeans or shorts, depending on the weather, and then go back home and get on with my writing. If I feel stuck or distracted, sometimes I go out and have a cup of coffee in a nearby café, on my own or with a friend. Or lately, I write to you.

I sometimes miss putting on nice clothes and make-up to go out to the office, but mostly I am content working at home in my jeans or sometimes even my flowery pyjamas. I am very grateful that I have the flexibility to be with my children on school-breaks or when they are sick, and I can work from home at all hours. If I don't get enough done during the day for one reason or another, I then work at night. Writing is a very important part of my life now, and I can't say that I miss the Diplomatic Service. The only thing I do miss is the people – some of them were really great. I'm sure you'd like them if you met them.

Now tell me, doesn't the fact you have to spend most holidays at your in-laws' affect your relationship with your own parents? Your mother doesn't mind that you don't come to celebrate with her? If you only knew what a big issue this is in our society . . . I think I've written about this before. I suppose it helps when there is a tradition and there are clear rules on this, but still, it seems unfair towards the women's families.

In that case, every mother has to pray for sons, so she is not left alone on the holidays!

By the way, in just a few short days it will be April 1st, or April Fool's Day, when we try to pull practical jokes on friends and family. Do you have this in Palestine? Most people here actually forget about it, which is great, because then you can really fool them! Often pranks are pulled on radio and television here, too, which can be hilarious.

Yours,
Daniela

* * *

April 5th, 2009
Ramallah

Hello Daniela,

I hope you had an amusing April Fool's Day! We do something similar on May 1st.

You asked me in one of your previous letters about life for young women here – about what happens if a young woman falls in love with a man. So maybe I should write about that today.

To begin with, things differ somewhat from place to place and family to family. Falling in love is not a crime, but we have clear lines. For example, I fell in love with my husband when I met him, and we dated for a while, for about six months. We went out in the company of friends and relatives, we always went to public places and, most importantly, my family knew about it.

Some families wouldn't allow their daughter to go out with a man unsupervised. Like in every community, different people have different ideas about how things should be done.

We used to have a neighbour who was particularly tough on his daughters. He didn't let them do anything. My father was more understanding – we were able to discuss things with him and he never made decisions for us without consulting us first.

He would try to convince us that he was right, and we would try to convince him that we were right. Usually one side managed to convince the other. This is why my sister and I respect our family; they always respected us. My mother was the tougher of the two parents, and many times I chose to ask my dad for permission to do things. If I wanted to go on a trip, to come back late or go on a course or a meeting where there were boys and girls together, my mother used to say "no" and he used to say "yes". When my mother forbade me from going somewhere or doing something I wanted to do, my father sometimes managed to convince her to change her mind. He always said that children need to be trusted and respected, so they in turn learn the same trust and respect.

This was very true for us, Daniela. He gave us relative freedom to do the things we wanted to do, and this

111

motivated us to respect our family and its rules. The neighbour's daughters, on the other hand . . . they were under so much pressure and had so many prohibitions that they enjoyed doing the things they were forbidden to do.

If a young woman sees or meets a man she likes, she can usually find a way to get to know him – in an indirect way. The same for a man; if he sees a girl he likes and wants to meet, he should find someone who knows her and who can introduce them as if by chance. And there are many other tricks like this.

The 'reputation' you have as a young woman is very important, and you need to take good care of it. You can't be seen wandering around town with various men – you'll never find a husband this way, even if you did nothing wrong!

I have a good friend who studied engineering at university and who is very successful professionally, but she is over thirty and still single, which is unusual in Palestine. And perhaps this has something to do with the fact that she always hung around with male students. I am sure it really was only for the purpose of studying, but still – our society doesn't see it this way. It is not very forgiving towards young women who are liberated and successful. What to do?

I'd like to know what is it like in your society – does the family have a say in when a girl chooses her partner? Does the community put any limitations on a girl's behaviour?

Kisses,
Shireen

P.S. I am not ignoring the story you told me about David. I just don't know what to say, except that it is so sad and painful. There are so many terrible stories, on both sides.

CROSSING QALANDIYA

April 10th, 2009
Tel Aviv

Hello Shireen,

Yesterday we celebrated the Jewish Passover with our extended families, and it was a wonderful opportunity to tell all those who still haven't heard of you about our exchange. I had mostly enthusiastic reactions (only one or two cynical ones) and I enjoyed telling everyone about how we met and about our developing friendship.

Perhaps you know that the celebration of the Jewish Passover commemorates the exodus of the people of Israel from Egypt. They were slaves to the pharaoh and, according to the Old Testament, God (with the kind assistance of Moses) took them out of Egypt. After a little stroll in the desert, which took about forty years, he brought them to The Promised Land – Canaan. One of my favourite jokes is that Moses had a stutter, and it was all just one big misunderstanding. He really wanted God to take the people of Israel to Canada, but he just said "Ca.. ca.. ca.." and God guessed Canaan. And that is how we ended up here, fighting for our existence ever since.

God not only helped the people of Israel escape slavery in Egypt; he also punished the enslaving Egyptians with the ten plagues. He then led us through the Red Sea which, according to the story, parted, and all the Jews walked through it to dry land. When the Egyptian soldiers tried to chase the escaping slaves, the sea closed down on them and they all drowned. Nice story.

113

Many believe that this is the way things really happened, and it is tradition to tell this story in detail around the Passover dinner table, for the benefit of the young generation. We read a book called *Hagada*, which tells the story of the exodus from Egypt, and usually spend the entire evening reading, eating and drinking.

During the seven days of Passover we don't eat bread or anything made with yeast. This is because when the people of Israel were roaming the desert they could not stay long enough in one place to bake with yeast and let their bread rise. So we eat thin, unleavened bread called *matza*, and it's quite delicious with butter, chocolate spread or even stirred in crumbs into scrambled eggs. Do you ever eat *matza*? I would love you to come and celebrate Passover with us one day, at my mother's home. Perhaps some time will have to pass before you can accept this invitation, but I know the day will come when you will be able to join us for the festive dinner.

My impression from your last letter is that it is not easy to be a young woman in your society. Our society is very, very different – at least the secular society because, of course, religious families have very differently defined customs, quite similar to yours. But I grew up in a secular environment, and there is absolutely no problem in going out with a guy you like. Fifteen year old girls dress up and look twenty and, frankly, parents of young girls probably do have quite a lot to worry about!

Of course, good education and common sense are important, and I very much agree with your father that young people should be trusted and respected, so they can prove that they are worthy of that respect and trust. I am just glad that I have two boys – perhaps I have less to worry about than if I had girls.

But parents to boys have other things to worry about – mainly the issue of military service. Unfortunately for us, and for you as well, all healthy eighteen year olds have to serve in the army. I am sure it is difficult for you to see these soldiers – who sometimes seem to be controlling your lives – as sons to parents who sit at home and worry about them, but this is also what they are.

In our culture, serving in the army is part of the experience of growing up for young men. It is here that they make friends and establish the contacts that will serve them for their entire lives. I honestly think that the majority of eighteen year olds do not fully comprehend the significance of what they are about to do when they go to the army. How can they? They are so young.

I am sure you've heard of those few who refuse to serve in the Occupied Territories – your territories. These are mostly older men, reservists, who can understand and see things in a slightly different way from most eighteen year olds. They refuse for reasons of ideology, and are even prepared to go to jail for their beliefs. They call themselves "conscientious objectors" and there are more and more of them around. Of course, they are heavily criticised by many in Israeli society, those who still believe that serving in the Palestinian Territories serves the interests of Israel.

Most young people know that they are risking being labelled disloyal citizens, or even cowards, if they refuse to serve in the Occupied Territories, so they do what they are told. And between us, what do eighteen year olds really know about life?

In a way, this is not so different from the bad reputation young women in your society risk if they hang out with male friends. There can be finger-pointing and accusations, and even discrimination when they try and get jobs in the future. It is awful, don't you think?

When I think of the way our society could have evolved if we didn't have to worry about our security and invest so much in the military, I feel a real heart-ache. How much blood and pain is still necessary until both sides be able to understand that this is a lose-lose situation?

Here I am, sliding into politics again, when we are actually discussing young women in our societies and what they can and cannot do. It isn't that they are allowed to do anything and everything here; of course there are some social limits. But even here the army plays an important role. Unfortunately, it plays an important role in almost every aspect of our lives.

If someone at eighteen is old enough to go to the army and to risk their life, then they are old enough to do other things, too – aren't they? This is the way most young people see it, anyway.

What else can I tell you? In this aspect, we live in very different societies, but I suspect that a lot of it is because I grew up in a secular world. I am sure that religions contain a lot of important and clever ideas that are designed to keep the moral order in society, but what upsets me most is the inequality between men and women that seems to come hand in hand with it. Yes, I know some will say it is not discrimination – that men are just different from women. To me this is just an excuse.

Do you know that in Judaism one of the thanks men give in prayer is "Thank you, God, for not making me a woman"?! What is more discriminatory than this? Even if in the past women needed men to protect them, today the situation is very different. Women are stronger – not just physically, but mentally and professionally, too, and they can do just fine on their own. These ancient rules were made for men's sake, not women's. I really think it is time they changed.

I am not a bra-burning feminist, but I certainly think women can and should have equal rights to men. It is awful that they have to worry so much about their reputation, while men are permitted to do anything they want. I hope these lines will not upset you, but I feel now that we can be open with each other and share our real thoughts. I think of you as a close friend these days.

Would you have believed, if someone told you a year ago when we met in Geneva, that we could become such good friends?

Yours,
Daniela

★   ★   ★

April 15th, 2009
Ramallah

Dear Daniela,

My pen seems to have gone on strike. I really want to write to you, but I cannot decide where to start. I am sure you've had this feeling, too, being a writer. Ever since I was a little girl I've wanted to write, but found I couldn't. Even today I often find it hard to express myself.

I miss my mother very much. I am in Ramallah, and she is in Nablus. I would like so much to be able to hug and kiss her, but when we're together I don't do it. Even as a little girl, I found it hard. It must be a matter of personality, because my younger brother has no problem with physical affection. When I see them, I am envious of how easy it seems for him.

I think I should work on developing my feelings and the way I express them. I always say it, but find it very hard to do. And I miss my parents so much. It feels as if they are very far away. True, it is not so far in a direct line, and if we had normal roads with normal traffic it would take me half an hour to get to them. But the road-blocks and check-points make everything very difficult.

You can't imagine how much my mother suffers every time she comes to visit me. Sometimes I cry for her, for what she has to go through, especially because she never comes empty-handed. She always brings foods and drinks I like, and fills up my fridge with the wonderful things she cooks and bakes for us. She comes to visit us about once a month, and carries her bags – sometimes through the hills – in order to get to the other side of the Hawara check-point. When the check-point is closed, which it often is, she arrives all dusty with mud-stained clothes. I always beg her not to bring all these things for me, as it is much easier to get to Ramallah from Nablus if you don't have anything with you. And even when the Hawara check-point is open, there is a fifteen-minute walk from one side to the other, and someone always goes through her stuff and asks her what is she bringing and who she is bringing it for – all sorts of unpleasant questions. I wish she didn't have to go through all this.

But you know how mothers are – or perhaps they are not all the same. My neighbour tells me that her mother is always asking to have things brought to her. But in our family, my mother is always the one to bring me food, presents, all sorts of things. *Inshallah*, I wish to God, Daniela, that I can be like her for my children one day. There's nothing like a loving mother to enrich one's life, and there's no one who could take her place.

The funny thing is that every time I talk about her, she calls or sends me a text. She sent me one just now, asking how I am.

I believe that when you really love someone, they can feel it. In my language there is an expression that says all hearts are tied together – *al kulub khawater*.

Maybe I've already mentioned this, but do you know that many times I've dreamed of things that have later happened. It is weird and I have no explanation for it, but it happens.

Look how much I've written – and only half an hour ago I didn't know what to write. Can you imagine how long this letter would have turned out if I'd had a plan?

Salam *and kisses to you, my dear.*
Shireen

*   *   *

April 21st, 2009
Tel Aviv

Hello Shireen,

I so enjoyed reading your last letter. I truly recognised myself in it. I, just like you, can't always express my feelings when I want to. Especially towards my mother – whom I love and appreciate so much – but when she is next to me, I find it difficult to show how I feel.

I was shocked to read about what your mother has to go through to get to you, carrying food and gifts, because I know my mother would do exactly the same thing if she were in your mother's place. She would have to go through the same unpleasantness. It is really hard to comprehend, and to accept.

Yes, we always have the issue – or excuse – of our own security. And it is true that even women have been caught carrying and smuggling explosives. But still. As long as mothers cannot carry food for their children without going through hell, nothing can truly change.

My mother is a very active woman, and she's always been that way. Despite having taken early retirement, she continues to work as an architect and gets a lot of pleasure from it. I admire her, and I am sure she doesn't even know it – because I never tell her. It is you that has made me realise this, and I really should do something about it.

I wonder how our mothers would get along if they ever met. Could they become friends, like us? Of course, there is the language barrier. But just as we've found a way around it with a third language, and just as we seem to have overcome our cultural barriers (which we slowly discover are not so great) and find a common language, perhaps they could, too. Maybe one day, when there are fewer walls and barriers and road-blocks and check-points, and when fewer permits are necessary, we could introduce them to one another?

After all, you don't need more than one friend from 'the other side' to realise that we are very much alike. Israelis and Palestinians just seem to see the opposite sides of the same coin, as we say in Hebrew.

Your father sounds like a wonderful person, too. I think he'd get along well with my dad. So, how would your family react if you suggested that they meet an Israeli family? I am sure there are many who would enjoy meeting families on the other side, especially among the younger generation. I wouldn't be too surprised if, in a decade, friendships like ours are commonplace.

And there's one more important thing that I mustn't forget to tell you – I've decided to learn Arabic. True, some schools in Israel teach Arabic to kids, but the truth is that despite the fact it is supposed to be our second official language, very few Israelis speak it.

So I've decided it is important that I learn it, so one day I can speak to you in your own language. Next week I'll be starting a weekly Arabic course. I hope you can help me with my homework?!

Yours,
Daniela

* * *

Daniela Norris and Shireen Anabtawi

April 27th, 2009
Ramallah

Dear Daniela,

I hope my letter finds you and your family in good health.

We are all well. Yesterday my husband's sister gave birth to a baby girl. She had an easy birth, thank God, and she didn't have an epidural, because her mother – my mother-in-law – told her that it might cause her back pains later . . . She said the same to me before I gave birth. But, of course, I didn't listen.

You know, sometimes older people do give good advice. I say 'sometimes', because not everything they say is true. I don't know if it's the same in your society, but in ours, when an older person says something, we don't argue. We'd never tell them to their face if they were wrong. We sit quietly and wait for them to finish what they have to say – this is part of our culture.

I just remembered an amusing story to do with the generation gap. My paternal grandfather is eighty-five years old, God bless and protect him. And until this very day, he still treats my father as if he is his little boy, and always tells him: "The age gap between us always stays the same; it never shrinks."

And my father still looks up to his father. He would never raise his voice when talking to him, and always treats his opinions with much respect.

Once my father was in the shop my grandfather owns and it was full of customers. My brother was seventeen at the time, and he was there, too, helping out. My grandfather gets

122

angry very easily these days (as many older people do) and told my father off for something, in front of everyone.

And who came to my father's defence? My little brother, of course. He said to our grandfather: "Why do you talk to my father this way in front of other people?" and then stormed out of the shop. He came home crying, but as soon as he came in and before my mother could ask him what happened, the phone rang. It was my grandfather – calling to apologise to my brother. He didn't feel the need to apologise to his son, my father – but to my brother! Imagine that.

Times are changing, and they are about to change even more. Both my grandfather and my father told me that if they ever saw one of their school-teachers coming towards them on the street, they would cross to the other side, to show respect. These days, it is the teachers who cross the street, in fear of their students. There is not enough respect towards teachers these days. Only God knows what else will change in these crazy times.

Yours,
Shireen

★   ★   ★

May 3rd, 2009
Tel Aviv

Hello Shireen,

How are you and how is your family?

Spring has finally arrived, and I am enjoying the warm weather. It's the same every year; when winter is about to end I can hardly wait until summer, and in the middle of summer I am already counting the days until winter. But I am always content in spring and autumn – I love the moderate seasons. They give me the feeling that everything is full of potential, and anything can happen.

I wish that in our society the elderly were as respected as they are in yours. Yes, it is in our religion and our tradition, but the reality is somewhat different. There are many elderly people living on their own, without anyone to take care of them. For some of them, this is because they have no children or other close family, but for others, it is because their kids and families are too busy to look after them.

On the other hand, it is often the case that elderly people who have prejudices about multiple issues feel they have the right to tell everyone how things should be, and go around instructing younger people on how they should think or behave. I do agree that wisdom comes with age and, in many cases, elderly people are also wise. But you know, I also believe that we have the right to make our own mistakes and, of course, pay the price for those mistakes.

But it is important to give elderly people the feeling they are being respected. It must be terrible to go through your whole life, and at the end of it have to cope with youngsters who think they know everything better than you do. And what breaks my heart most is elderly people who come here from other countries, and suddenly have to adapt to a completely new reality, a completely different culture. They usually leave their homelands because they are being persecuted there, or because of economic need; or sometimes it is because they are lonely and are joining family in Israel. But this does not make the transition any easier. It is much harder than moving to a new country when you are still young and strong.

It is good that your grandfather understood that his disrespect of your father actually hurt his grandchild, too. So who is right? I vote for your brother, who sounds like a clever and courageous young man. But I am sure that your grandfather is very wise, and it is just the impatience that sometimes comes with age that caused him to react the way he did towards your father, his own son.

And teachers . . . teachers are an entirely different story. Students in Israel don't respect their teachers half as much as they should. Even when I was at school – more than twenty years ago – it was considered acceptable fun to pull practical jokes on teachers. When I think of it today, I feel ashamed. Why were we so horrible to them?

The teaching profession here suffers from a mediocre image and many talented people turn to other professions, even if they could have become good and influential teachers. But still, there are many wonderful teachers out there, and they deserve to be appreciated. The whole attitude that many young people in the so-called developed world suffer from – where they are doing someone a favour by going to school – is very wrong. And again, it goes back to the education they are getting at home.

And I think the whole world is going through a similar process. I don't know if it is modernisation or globalisation, but in more traditional societies – like your own – elderly people and teachers are shown so much more respect. I think this is truly enviable.

I wonder how our own kids will treat us in thirty or forty years. I think a lot of it depends on how we are treating and educating them today. Don't you agree?

Yours,
Daniela

* * *

May 8th, 2009
Ramallah

Dear Daniela,

How are you and your family? We are well, thank God.

I've been exhausted lately. As my children grow older, I seem to have more and more duties and assignments. They have all sorts of activities – play-dates, birthday parties, never-ending appointments – and it is me who has to take care of it all. Buy gifts, drive them there, pick them up. It makes me very, very tired. You know, I have lost quite a bit of weight lately. Sometimes I just don't have time to eat.

We are in the second week of May, and just like you play tricks on people on April 1st, we do it in early May. It is called *kizbaat nissan* – 'the lie of the month of Nisaan'. And believe me, I am fed up with trying to tell the difference between truths and lies. Even when someone greets me with a "good morning" on the street, I am suspicious.

During this time, children, adults and old people alike turn lying into an artform, and this can cause many problems. Would you believe that many women get divorced because of *kizbaat nissan*? Please don't laugh, I am totally serious.

I try lying sometimes, but it doesn't come easily. Everyone can see it on my face when I lie, and this always works against me. I can never pretend. Oh well, let's move on to a more interesting subject – you and your life.

I'd like to know more about you and your children; about the daily duties you have. Are they as heavy as mine? Does your husband sometimes act like a third child, too? I cook, I clean, I wash and I iron for three kids. Do you do the same? Does your husband help around the house?

By the way, this is something that I wanted to ask you a long time ago – how did you meet your husband? And how did you decide to get married? I am curious to know whether this is something that differs a lot between our two societies.

Awaiting your letter!

Yours,
Shireen

★   ★   ★

May 15th, 2009
Tel Aviv

Shalom Shireen,

I hope you are well. When I read your last letter I really felt your exhaustion. Yes, things are somewhat similar here, but I really can't complain that my husband doesn't help around the house, because he does. Even when he comes home late from work, he bathes the kids, and sometimes even makes dinner or washes dishes. What can I say? I am a lucky girl. I know that not all men are like that.

However, in our generation and in our society, men are definitely expected to help around the house and look after and spend time with the children.

Ron, who is only five and a half, suddenly has afternoon activities and birthday parties and all sorts of other things, and of course, I am his chauffeur. I do have two girl friends with children of similar ages and we help each other out. Don't you have one or two friends who could at least share the burden of shuttling the kids around?

Of course, the older they get, the more places they want to be chauffeured to, until they are seventeen and get their own drivers' licences. And then we'll have even more reasons to worry.

How did I meet my husband? It isn't a very complicated story. I met him at a friend's house and I liked him straight away. The problem was, I was with someone else at the time. Things weren't great with that other guy, so I left him and started going out with my future husband. Maybe this sounds very risqué to you, but it is common in our society. And it is not uncommon to have several boyfriends and live with someone before you decide to marry them.

When we decided to get married, we informed our parents, who were very happy for us. By then we had been together for a couple of years, and we lived together. Fortunately, my parents liked him from the very beginning, because once I had a boyfriend they really didn't like. I still went out with him. In retrospect, they were right. But nothing really bad came out of it, except for some heartache.

In our secular society it doesn't really matter how many boyfriends you've had before you decide to marry someone, though everything has a limit, of course, I am not talking about dozens of boyfriends, but a few between high-school and marriage is definitely common practice!

There are some who do marry their first boyfriend or girlfriend, but they are the exception. We also have a very high divorce rate, possibly because people know they have other choices, which makes it easier to leave your spouse if things are really bad.

There is also the silly issue of being married before you're thirty, which I find a bit ridiculous. In our society, if you don't marry before you're thirty, people think it likely that you won't get married at all. But this, too, is changing and becoming more like Europe, where people marry older (and have fewer children, respectively). In Europe, too, more and more people live together without being married, and even have children together, and this is becoming more and more common in Israel.

So the answer is that our societies are quite different in this respect, but, as I keep saying, possibly because I grew up in a non-religious family and environment. When you have your own state perhaps some things will change in your society too, although I am sure there will be many who will object to these changes.

I wouldn't be surprised if in the future there are more 'mixed' couples – Israeli and Palestinian. Yes, there are some even today, but society looks at them as an anomaly. What would happen, for example, if someone in your family wanted to marry an Israeli? Is this even a possibility?

In Israel we do have intermarriages – mostly between Jews and Christians – and the secular society doesn't make a big deal out of it. However, the Jewish identity of Israel

Daniela Norris and Shireen Anabtawi

as a state is very important to the vast majority of Israelis. Of course, non-Jews can, and do, live here and practise their religions, but Israel is the only state in the world that has Jewish characteristics and where Jews can come to live simply because they are Jews. This is a result of the Holocaust, where six million Jews were murdered, and when the state of Israel was founded in 1948, it was founded as the safe home for the Jews who could return to it after a bitter tragedy and two thousand years of living in exile among non-Jews.

There are not many marriages between Jews and Muslims – I'd guess because there is so much tension and so many psychological barriers. As you know, what matters to me is the person and not his or her religion. There are many Israelis, and others, who would disagree with me, of course. But I am curious to know your opinion on this issue of intermarriage.

And please, tell me how you met your husband.

Yours,
Daniela

* * *

May 22nd, 2009
Ramallah

Dear Daniela,

How are you? I hope all is well with you and your family. I enjoyed reading your last letter, and learning more about you and your life. I am well, and so is my husband. Perhaps I'll start my letter by telling you how we met.

130

It was also easy and simple, like in your case. I met him when I was twenty-three, when I went to apply for a job and he interviewed me. It was love at first sight – and he asked me to come in for a follow-up interview!

I did come for the follow-up, and during the interview felt he was eyeing me in a strange way. He started talking about things that had nothing to do with work, and when the interview ended, he asked whether he could call me later to give me a final answer. He did call me that same day – several times! He wanted to know that I made it safely back from Ramallah to Nablus, that I was feeling ok, and more and more excuses.

The next morning, he called me again, and asked whether I could come again to Ramallah that same day. He needed to see me urgently, he said. I said that I would try to come, but I didn't even know if the road was open that morning. (Sometimes portions of that road are closed because of the road-blocks and check-points.)

I dressed myself nicely, put on some make-up and told my parents that I needed to go to Ramallah again, for work reasons. Then I went out to look for a taxi that would take me there. Every single driver said that the road was closed that morning, until I eventually found one who agreed to go. I waited until he had six other passengers to fill his taxi, and we headed off.

It should normally take thirty minutes to get from Nablus to Ramallah. That day it took us three-and-a-half hours. When we reached Ramallah, it was already afternoon.

On the way, he called several times on my mobile, asking whether I was on my way and what was going on. And when I finally entered his office, I discovered that nothing urgent was waiting, he just wanted to see me again. I sat on the chair in front of him, and he asked my permission to close the door, so we could talk privately. I asked him to leave it ajar, and he respected my request, of course.

He started talking, and didn't stop for an hour. He told me how much he liked me, and I just sat there quietly and listened. When he finished, he asked for my reaction to what he had just said, but what could I say? In our culture, as a woman, it is difficult to say what you think where these things are concerned. The man should always take the initiative. Of course, I did like him.

So I said I liked him, but that I had only known him for a couple of days, and if he had serious intentions he would first have to win my mother's heart. By the time we finished talking, it was dark outside. It was February, and it had just started raining.

He asked if he could accompany me back to Nablus in a taxi, because he didn't want me to take the trip on my own, in the dark. I said that he would have to ask my father for permission.

He immediately called my father, and apologised for keeping me so late in Ramallah. He asked for – and got – permission to travel alone with me in a taxi. Then he called a private cab from Jerusalem and we headed to Nablus together.

When we arrived, my parents thanked him for accompanying me, and invited him in for a cup of coffee. Of course, he accepted immediately.

My mother, who had rejected many, many potential suitors on the grounds that "she just didn't see my future with them" said that she liked him straight away. A few months later we were married, and the rest is history. So you see, despite all the constraints, we, too, have successful love stories.

I will end here, because I have to go and register my daughter Ghazal for summer camp. Her summer holiday starts next week.

Kisses,
Shireen

★   ★   ★

May 29th, 2009
Tel Aviv

Hello Shireen,

Thank you for your last letter – it was lovely to read about how you met your husband. It is a truly magical story. I have no doubt that love can overcome many obstacles, but I just wonder how many women in your society have the good fortune that you had? I hope the answer is 'many'.

This week we celebrated *Shavuot* – tabernacles. It is a celebration that I adore, largely because we get to eat mainly dairy products, fruit and vegetables. I don't remember if I've told you before that I was vegetarian for many years, and even today I prefer dairy to meat. I don't know whether you know that in our religion it is forbidden to eat the two at the same time. The original phrase in the Old Testament instructs that a lamb should not be cooked in its mother's milk, but rabbis have interpreted this more generally to mean that meat and dairy should never be mixed. And indeed, I recently read that there are health reasons to avoid eating the two together, as their digestion times vary.

Luckily for me, there is such a big choice of dairy produce in Israel, more than anywhere else I've been in the world. There are so many types of cheese and cheese-cakes . . . In short, this celebration is a real feast for me!

We celebrate *Shavuot* to commemorate the day when, according to our Torah, God gave Moses the Ten Commandments on Mount Sinai. It is one of the three festivities I told you about – together with *Sukkoth* and *Passover*. It also commemorates the end of *sfirat haomer*. Beginning on the second night of Passover, we count the days and weeks; a count that goes on for seven weeks, because it took seven weeks to reach Mount Sinai. The People of Israel escaped from Egypt on the 15th of Nissan, which is the first day of Passover. On the 6th of Sivan, celebrated ever since as the festival of *Shavuot*, they assembled at the foot of Mount Sinai and received the Torah from God.

I had to go and check exactly why we celebrate this holiday, so I could tell you. Would you believe I didn't know the exact reason?

This is partly because in the secular part of our society all this boils down to is a big celebration of the harvest, which has turned into quite a commercial affair. New dairy products are launched and there's a huge marketing campaign for various foodstuffs. However, this is what I miss most when I'm outside Israel – the Israeli cheeses. Do you eat a lot of dairy? Tell me more about what you like to eat. Of course, I hope that one day soon I will be able to come and see for myself. There's nothing like good food to bring people together.

Perhaps you've noticed that I am hungry. It is three-thirty in the morning and I can't sleep (maybe because I had too much cheese for dinner!) so I got up, made myself a cup of tea and sat down at the kitchen table and decided, instead of reading yesterday's paper – which is not very inspiring – to write to you. It's a much more pleasant thing to do.

I guess I should go back to bed, because in three hours I have to wake up and make sandwiches for Ron, who's going on a school trip. He's already told me what he'd like in his sandwiches – can you guess? Cheese, of course.

Yours,
Daniela

★　　★　　★

June 2nd, 2009
Ramallah

Dear Daniela,

A bit late, I know, but Happy *Shavuot*!

I, too, love cheese and a celebration of dairy sounds wonderful. We also have some amazing cheeses here in Palestine and I will tell you more about these later, but first I want to tell you about something else – something that bothers me a lot.

Yesterday we had a visit from my neighbour's daughter. She's been living in Geneva for the past seventeen years, and she told us about her children; my neighbour's grandchildren.

She was complaining about how they've been behaving – or, to be more precise – how they've been behaving because they live abroad.

Her eldest son has left his parents' house to live in an apartment on his own. Her daughter, who is eighteen, doesn't listen to her parents at all. Not only does she not listen, but she talks back and does the opposite of what she is being asked to do, or not to do.

But you know what? I really can't blame this young woman. I actually blame her mother. She is the one who left Palestine and went to live abroad. For many years she didn't think about keeping in regular touch with her family in Palestine. She raised her kids differently from the way children are being brought up here, and she chose to adopt a lifestyle different from ours. Of course, these choices now affect her children.

Many people who live outside their native land know how to keep in touch with their roots and their culture. And I think it is right that if someone chooses to live elsewhere, they should still teach their kids about their background. For example, this woman never taught her children to pray, to fast during Ramadan or to respect our holidays and traditions. Now, suddenly, she expects them to live abroad and still know and respect the ways of their people. She should have taught them about these things when they were young.

Now it is very difficult for her to control her children's behaviour and, to her, everything seems at odds with the world she grew up in. But it is too late. You know, I always try to talk to my kids about things of importance; I try to explain that there are many ways of living in this world, and that there are differences between countries and cultures.

When my six year old daughter sees women on television wearing bikinis, she asks, "Mother, why are they wearing that thing?"

I explain to her that even if it isn't considered respectable in our society to wear a bikini, it is fine in theirs. She understands and accepts this.

I think that if people raise their children this way, the children will grow up to be respectful of their own and other cultures. And they won't suffer from culture shock when exposed to new ways of life.

Yes, there are differences between peoples and lifestyles, but no one can say that one way of life is better than another. The more we know and appreciate what we have, the more we can ensure the continuity of our own culture.

I think that the main reason some people lose their way is an internal one – they mix between cultures and lose their own identity. This is a big problem here, especially among young people.

I am not sure why I am giving you this lecture, but I wanted to share this story with you, because it has been on my mind. And, since I am discussing tradition, here is a question I've been thinking about for some time now: I know that what keeps your people together are the Jewish religion and your historical roots. But people in Israel have come from different places, and I always wondered how you can live together with such a mix of cultures and traditions. If everyone has their own food, their own customs and their own rules, how do you bridge over these wide gaps?

I will end here – please write soon.

Yours,
Shireen

★ ★ ★

June 11th, 2009
Tel Aviv

Hello Shireen,

You have no idea how strange I feel lately – almost as if I've started seeing things differently – through your eyes. Maybe this is normal, because we know each other relatively well now, and of course this has an affect. I keep finding myself explaining 'your side' to people. And, frankly, I am shocked at some of the reactions I get.

There are many people here who are completely blind to the way things look from your point-of-view, and to what your people are going through. I am sure this is also true for some of the people on your side. But suddenly it has become clear to me that so many of our problems are the results of miscommunication and misunderstandings. Maybe it is naivety (as some of my people would surely say) or perhaps it is incredible injustice (as some of yours may claim), but I truly think that if only there was a way to walk in each other's shoes for a little while – to have a glimpse of how the world looks through the other person's eyes even for one day – many of these problems could be resolved. For example, the issue you raised in your last letter of people coming to Israel from all over the world.

Shireen, if they didn't have this country, where would they go? People who are persecuted for their religion, because of who they are – and true – there are also those who immigrate for economic or political reasons. But if they didn't have Israel, the same land their forefathers lived in so long ago, what would they do? You, as a Muslim, have other countries where you can live and feel part of the culture. I don't imply that because there are other Muslim countries you shouldn't have your own state – of course you should. But we, as Jews, simply don't have another state; a Jewish state where our holidays are the national holidays and the day of rest is Saturday, the Sabbath. This is why so many Jews, from all over the world, want to come here.

Now that I know you and you explain these things to me, of course I can better understand your frustration. But what can I do? I was born in my own skin – I am Jewish, I am the granddaughter of Holocaust survivors, and even if I am not at all religious and I believe that humanism is more important than religion and politics, of course my first concern is the security and future of my children. This is only human, and I am sure the same is true on your side.

So the only solution is dialogue. We need to talk about everything, constantly exchanging opinions and thoughts. And I would like you to promise me one thing: that no matter what happens between our peoples, we will always continue our own dialogue. And I hope that one day, in the not-too-distant future, we'll be able to have this dialogue face-to-face.

Yours,
Daniela

* * *

June 17th, 2009
Ramallah

Dear Daniela,

I hope you and your family are well.

I am writing to you from work, because I simply can't find quiet time at home lately. It is the summer holiday, and the kids are spending more time in the house. I am sure you know what it is like when everything gets turned upside-down! Still, I love coming home after a long day at work.

How is your summer holiday going? Will you be going away? We're staying here this summer. We were supposed to go to Jordan, to attend a relative's wedding, but just the thought of travelling from Ramallah to Amman with the kids makes me tired.

So, I would like to comment on some of the things you said in your last letter. You wrote that we have the option of living in other Muslim countries because we are Muslims. Well, it isn't so. Just like Israel is the only state for the Israelis, Palestine is the only state for us, Palestinians. I hope you are not forgetting, my friend, that this land is also the land of *our* forefathers.

You asked me in one of your last letters why we commemorate the *nakbah*, our disaster, when we were chased away from our lands and the State of Israel was founded. I haven't answered this question, because it is very difficult for me to believe that you really cannot see the reason. How can we be happy for you Israelis, rejoice that you have your own state, when we do not have our own? After all, the State of

140

Israel was founded on land taken away from Palestinians. Yes, this is something we can cope with in the future, once we have our own state. But in the meantime, we will only have our *nakbah*.

I'll give you a small example, which I hope will help clarify things. Can a Muslim go to his neighbour's house, and move in, just because they share the same religion?

What brings people together is not just their religion. In the U.S, for example, there are Christians, Muslims and Jews, and they all live together. What makes that possible is nationalism, not religion.

My people and I – Muslims and Christians alike – live in our county, on our land. I don't think we would be welcome in any other country if we stayed indefinitely. After all, guests who overstay their welcome get tedious. Everyone needs their own space, and even if your own mother came to visit and stayed for too long, she would feel unwanted after a while. You would want your privacy, wouldn't you?

The Palestinians who live outside Palestine are asking for the Right of Return, because they will never feel they are living in dignity unless they have the right to live on their own land, even if that land is occupied, my dear.

Do you know that Palestinians who live in certain countries cannot work as doctors or engineers even if they went to university in that same country? In other places, they are not even entitled to own a house.

I better finish here – our Director General is calling us to a meeting!

Kisses,
Shireen

* * *

June 23rd, 2009
Tel Aviv

Shireen *Shalom,*

Your last letter was extremely interesting for me to read. I can't say I knew all those things about Palestinians living in other countries, or about your *nakbah*. When you explain, I have to admit that they suddenly make some sense. I am glad you shared your point of view with me, because it is the first time I have come close to really understanding these things. But, I can't avoid going back to what is the main issue, as far as I am concerned: there isn't another Jewish state in the entire world. There isn't a place where Jews can have their religion, culture and customs as the national norm. So it's true that this isn't absolute justice, but there must be a better solution than what we are presently going through, right?

Our school year is ending later this week, and I already registered Ron and Ben to day-camps. What else can I do with them all summer? Yes, there are swimming pools and parks and television, of course, but it isn't enough. I think they need the company of other children, and not to stay home with their mum and bug her all day!

I don't know what your day-camps are like, but for Ben's age – three and a half – it is just a continuation of kindergarten, and it's even in the same place. They don't really take them out to different activities. The only real difference is that they get chocolate spread on their sandwiches, not only on Fridays, but in the middle of the week, too.

For Ron's age – nearly six – the camps are much more interesting. They shuttle them around to various activities and they really get a lot out of the summer months. In any case, they'll go to camp for the first month, and I'll take the second month off and do all sorts of things with them. Maybe we'll even go north for a week in August, where it is cooler. Tel Aviv in summer feels like being inside an oven.

Now, as the summer starts, the absurdity of our situation is even more pronounced. Why is it that two friends, with children of similar ages, who live an hour's drive from one another at the most, can't meet so their kids can play together? Of course I know the answer. But if before I met you I accepted it as an absolute fact . . . well, it isn't so easy to accept anymore.

Please tell me more about what you do in the summer months. I know that you can't go to the beach, because you don't have access to it (other than those who live in Gaza, I guess). But if you could go, would you? You have told me that when you were little, you used to go with your parents to walk along the beach in Natanya. And another question, which perhaps is silly – would you wear a swim-suit on the beach?

You probably know that the beaches here are full of girls and women in bikinis, but of course, those from a religious background act and dress differently. They even have separate beaches for men and women, which is a good solution. Then at least everyone can relax. I never went to one of these separate beaches, but I assume that everyone wears swim-suits there.

When I was in high-school I loved to go to the beach and sunbathe, sometimes after school, and sometimes –

dare I admit it – during school hours. Today I am not so keen on the beach – certainly not as keen as my husband is. He can spend hours surfing, and takes the kids for a dip in the water and a play in the sand, while I prefer to drink my ice-coffee and read or write in a beach-side café.

I just get so annoyed by the sand that goes everywhere, and the water isn't always clean and there are jelly-fish. In short, I've become spoiled! So, if you could come here, I'm not sure that our first stop would be the beach.

What would that first stop be? Good question. I have to think about it. There are so many things I would like to do with you. I'd like to introduce you to all my friends, for one.

Where would you take me if I came to visit you one of these summer days?

Yours,
Daniela

★ ★ ★

June 30th, 2009
Ramallah

Hello Daniela,

Today I would like to tell you about something that happened more than two years ago. I don't know why, but I suddenly remembered and would like to share it with you. This story proves that people are human, after all – but that the level of humanity can vary from one person to another.

A friend of one of my relatives drove from Ramallah to Hebron with her husband and two young daughters, aged five and seven. On the way, they passed some settlers, who started throwing stones at their car. One of the large stones hit her young daughter's head, and she started bleeding. This happened on an isolated road between the two towns, and there was nothing or no one around other than the stone-throwing settlers, who ran away.

The little girl continued to bleed from her head, and her parents were desperate. Suddenly, a military jeep drove past. The mother got out of the car with the little girl in her arms, and tried to stop the jeep. The jeep stopped, but the driver refused to get out or open the window – the soldiers have instructions not to stop or get out of any car on that road. She begged him, in tears, to help her daughter. He shook his head. He was not getting out. But suddenly the door opened on the passenger side, out stepped a soldier. He gave the little girl first aid and called an Israeli ambulance, which arrived promptly. This saved the little girl's life, although she spent the next month in hospital.

The soldier who helped her was a reservist, and he came to visit her in hospital several times, and even brought her presents. The girl's parents didn't know how to thank him. Every time he came they were beyond themselves with gratitude. In an interview this soldier gave on Israeli TV he was asked why he got out of the car despite clear military instructions. He said that at that very moment, the only thing he could think of was his own daughter, who was of a similar age. He could imagine it was her, bleeding on this isolated road. And that is why he didn't hesitate to get out and help the little Palestinian girl.

So you see, my dear, there are different degrees of humanity in people. Can you imagine what could have happened if this specific soldier hadn't been there, in the right place, at the right time? What if only the soldier who refused to open the door had been there? This little girl probably wouldn't be alive today.

I intended to write to you about our summer activities, and about things I would do with you had you come to visit, but the kids are now driving me crazy. I need to get them out of the house, so I'll use the opportunity and take a walk with them to the post office, and post this letter. I promise that in the next I will write to you about all the things that we could do here.

> *Yours,*
> *Shireen*

★   ★   ★

> *July 7th, 2009*
> *Tel Aviv*

Dear Shireen,

Thank you for your last letter. I was deeply touched by the story. And it did sound familiar. I think I must have heard about it in the news some time ago, but probably didn't really pay attention. What can I say? It is so different hearing this story from you. I just hope there are many soldiers like that out there, men and women who can display not only their humanity but also their courage and individual thinking. Being human means sometimes listening to your heart, and following it. Never mind what your head and your fears tell you.

It is so hot today I felt sorry for my boys and let them continue sleeping in the air-conditioned room, rather than wake them up and take them out into the sizzling heat to camp. I will probably regret this later, when they start nagging me and won't let me work. But that's ok – this is how things are when you work from home, and one of the main reasons I decided to work from home was the kids, so why am I complaining?

When I was a student at university I also worked from home – I translated television programmes and films from English into Hebrew subtitles. Already back then I had discovered the joy of working in my pyjamas, just as I am now writing these lines. I used to spend entire nights in front of the computer screen – both studying and working – because I preferred doing other things during the day. So yes, just like everything else, working from home has advantages and disadvantages.

It is Tuesday today, and only one week into the school holidays, but the summer always has a different feeling to it, as if time slows down. Perhaps it is all in my head. Even the air has a different smell; of pollen and a certain stickiness, mixed with the fragrance of optimism. What is the connection between all these things? Perhaps it is the long days, or the fact that more people spend more time outdoors and things are happening all around me. Do you think I am strange?

Tomorrow I'll be taking the boys to a play – 'Uzu and Muzu From Kakaruzu.' I am sure you remember the story; it is the book I sent Ghazal for her last birthday (which reminds me of two things: soon it will be her birthday again, and that we've been corresponding for over a year!). It is the story of two brothers who loved each other very much, until they fought over something stupid and decided to stop talking. They built a high wall between their houses and told their children and their grandchildren that a scary, evil monster lived on the other side of the wall. For many generations no one bothered to check if this story was true, until a little boy climbed up onto the wall and saw a pretty little girl on the other side. Then everyone discovered that the stories they were told about each other were much exaggerated and there was no monster and no need for a wall.

What amazes me is that this story was written by Ephraim Sidon, one of our most talented writers, in the 1970s. This was many years before there was a wall – or maybe this is what gave them the idea?

The same writer wrote many Israeli comedies, and one of the funniest is called 'Hahartzufim' – a satire starring puppets that are all politician lookalikes. Perhaps we could convince this writer to write something funny about Israeli-Palestinian relations? It is true that many things are too painful to laugh about, but on the other hand, I think we've already agreed in the past that humour can bring people together. And there are still some things which can, and should be, approached with a little laughter.

Anyway, this Uzu and Muzu story has made a big comeback, and the present generation of children all know it. I have no doubt that they will be the ones to destroy the wall, just like in the story. I really regret that you are not able to join us tomorrow and come and see this play. I know you wouldn't have understood most of it, because it is in Hebrew, but still, I would have liked you to come. You said you speak a few words in Hebrew – do your kids speak a few words, too?

I do speak a little Arabic, but I know that I wouldn't be able to understand an entire play.

Well, I can hear my boys calling me – so they are awake now and the quiet time is over. I better go and check on them.

Please write soon!

Yours,
Daniela

★ ★ ★

July 14th, 2009
Ramallah

Dear Daniela,

My summer days are very similar to yours. We go to the swimming pool and play areas, despite the fact that there are only a few, and they are crowded and not very inspiring. My little boy, Saif, also goes to the same kindergarten he goes to for the rest of the year, so there's no big difference for him. Ghazal, who is nearly seven now, is going to camp every day. She has lunch there and does different activities every day, so I think we both have a very similar situation.

Now, what would we do if you came to visit? First, I'd like you to see my house, because I absolutely love it. I adore the furniture and rugs we've chosen, which are all antique-style. I would also like to take our kids to play in the park together, and have coffee with you while they play. Then we'd go for a drive around Ramallah, and I'd show you all the beautiful houses and restaurants that we have here.

I would probably ask some of my girl friends to come to the Plaza Mall, which is the only shopping centre we have at the moment (although some others are being constructed). There is a nice, large play-area there, and we could let the kids mess around while having another coffee, this time with my friends.

Then I'd probably take you to Nablus, to meet my family. You know, I don't want to repeat things that I have written about in the past, because what I'd like most is for you to come and see for yourself. Now enough 'what ifs'. Back to reality.

I like the Uzu and Muzu story very much. It is a tale for our time.

Yours,
Shireen

★ ★ ★

July 20th, 2009
Tel Aviv

Hello Shireen,

Last night I dreamt about you. Really, I dreamt that I was coming to visit you, and Ben jumped on Ghazal (he still remembers her, you know. When he sees her picture he says that this is his friend, Ghazal. He's only three and a half, but I think you're going to have to watch out for her when they meet . . . she's gorgeous).

Anyway, I dreamt that we were sitting in your kitchen and having coffee (in my dream, your kitchen had

Jerusalem-stone style tiles – and I don't even know if you live in a house or in an apartment). And you know something? I decided that I'd really like us to meet again. I would love to introduce you to all my friends, most of whom have never met a Palestinian.

Firstly, I'd like you to come to my place. We live in an apartment, so once we'd had a drink and our kids had started making too much noise, we'd take them out to the park. There's a big patch of grass and a play area, and they'd be able to run around and burn off some energy. I could ask my friends to come with their kids and meet us at this park, so you could all get to know each other. After a few hours with the kids, I'd ask my mum to come by – firstly to meet you, but also to look after the children for a bit so we could go out without them.

It would be great to hang out together, just you and me. We'd go to the shopping mall and look around, have a quiet cup of coffee. Then you'd also be able to feel how unpleasant it is every time you go into a shopping mall (or anywhere, for that matter) and everyone's bags have to be inspected, in case someone decides to carry a bomb inside or blow themselves up. This has happened several times in shopping centres.

Then I'd like to take you for a drive or a walk around Tel Aviv, just so you can see how we live our everyday lives. But for you, Jerusalem might be more interesting. So you'd have to stay another day, so we could visit Jerusalem. I have many friends there, too, since I used to work there, so we could go and see them the following day. After our drive or stroll in Tel Aviv, we'd come back home and make dinner for the kids, bathe them and go to sleep early, so we could wake up early the next morning and go.

I imagine you've been to Jerusalem in the past, but I don't know how well you know it. To be honest, I don't know Jerusalem that well. I was always more the Tel Aviv type, and there's a big difference in our society between 'Tel Aviv people' and 'Jerusalem people'. 'Tel Aviv people' tend to be more outgoing and into the party scene, and 'Jerusalem people' more laidback and studious – to roughly generalise, of course! We could meet one of my good friends who lives there, and she'd show us around. And from Jerusalem, you wouldn't be that far from your house in Ramallah . . . so near, yet so far.

There are many other places I'd like to take you, like the Dead Sea, the Galilee, even Eilat, all the way down south. You've probably never been to Eilat, right on the border with Egypt and by the shore of the Red Sea. However, going there in summer is not a good idea – the heat is unbearable.

So you see, there's so much we could do together, and it would be such great fun if you could come and see how things look from this side, even for just a short stay. And of course, I'd be thrilled to come and visit you, too. What do you say? I'm serious!

Yours,
Daniela

* * *

July 28th, 2009
Ramallah

Dear Daniela,

You know, I, too, am a little tired of this
correspondence. My hand is starting to hurt! Yes, I would
really like it if we could meet, together with our kids, before
the end of the summer. I haven't seen you for over a year.
Do you think our kids will remember each other? I think
mine will, because I always talk about you.

So, where shall we meet?

You know I can't come over to you easily, and you can't
come over to me. Let me think about it, and try to find a
solution. Of course, it would be wonderful to see you even if
we can't come to each other's houses. The key thing is that
we try and do it before the end of the summer, because then
the holiday will end and another busy school year will start.

By the way, I have been to many of the places you
mentioned in your letter, but it was a very long time ago.
Probably over twenty years ago. Every weekend we used to
go somewhere different. Of course, my younger brothers
who are eleven and sixteen have never been to any of these
places. After the 1988 *intifada* it became very difficult to get
into Israel. But before 1988, we'd often go to the Sahne
springs and to Tiberius and, of course, I've been to Ein Gedi
and the Dead Sea.

I just remembered that one time, when we went to the
Dead Sea, one of my relatives jumped into the water, head
first. She didn't imagine that the water would be that salty, and
of course her eyes didn't stop burning for a very long time!

I also know Natanya, Haifa and Akko – we used to visit Akko quite often, because we all loved it.

Ok then, I will leave it to you to suggest a date for our meeting – a meeting that I very much look forward to.

Yours,
Shireen

★   ★   ★

August 4th, 2009
Tel Aviv

Shireen,

You have no idea how happy your letter made me. Do you think we can really do this – meet up again? Even if we can't spend a couple of days together, as we'd like, I would at least like to see you and your children. A year is a very long time; my kids have changed quite a lot, and I'm sure yours have, too.

I would like my children to get to know our Palestinian friends for themselves, and not form an opinion based solely on what they see in the media and on television, and from what they hear from people on the street. I don't know if we will be able to get all the necessary permits to come and visit each other in our own homes, but there must be a neutral place where we could meet, even if for a short while?

You're right, if we are serious about this, we should do it before the end of the summer, before the end of the month. With everything that is going on around us, I have the feeling that we – all of us – are nearing the point of no return. We are at a point where something must be done; something needs to be changed right away. So maybe, to symbolise this, we could try and meet on the last Saturday of August, the 29th? Maybe because it is a Saturday, it will be easier to get through, from you to me or from me to you. If I remember correctly, it will also be just a few days after Ghazal's seventh birthday, and I would like to give her a birthday present in person. This way she'd know that it is from Ron and Ben, her Israeli friends.

So yes, absolutely. If you can make it, let's try and meet on Saturday, August 29th. The only question is where and how. If we plan to meet early in the morning, let's make it somewhere where we could at least talk face to face, and perhaps things will evolve from there. If they let me cross over, I'll come back with you to your house – after all, it can't be more than an hour away. And if they let you cross into Israel, then we'll go to my place. And if they don't let us cross at all, at least we'll be able to see each other!

What do you think? I am tired of writing letters. I want to see you.

Daniela

★ ★ ★

August 10th, 2009
Ramallah

Dear Daniela,

Very well, August 29th is the last weekend of the summer holiday. The kids go back to school on September 1st.

As far as a meeting place goes, I'm a bit stuck. Maybe we could meet at a check-point, but I don't know how easy that would be, and if there's any risk in it for you. My children and I are used to these places by now, but for you and your children, it may be a new and very unpleasant experience.

I think that the nearest and most convenient check-point to meet at would be Qalandiya, between Jerusalem and Ramallah. Maybe we can meet there, on that day? What time would suit you? I am not working on Saturdays, so I could make it in the morning. Let me know.

Yours,
Shireen

★ ★ ★

August 17th, 2009
Tel Aviv

Shireen,

Could this be my last letter before our meeting? I gave you my mobile number in Geneva, and it hasn't changed. I will give it to you again, just in case.

It is funny that for the past year I have felt no need to try and talk to you on the phone. The truth is that I generally dislike talking on the phone, and always have. I like to write, and I express myself better in writing. It is also easier, of course, because when we talk we have the language barrier. With all the trouble the British have caused in our region, at least they left us their language . . .

CROSSING QALANDIYA

So, as you suggested, Saturday morning at the Qalandiya check-point, at ten? The truth is I've never been there, and I don't know what to expect. Can you tell me a little more about it? What should I bring, in case they do let me through and I can come and meet your family? I would like to bring some gifts for them – what do they like? Is there anything I can bring from here; something you don't have over there?

What else can I say? That I really, really look forward to seeing you. I am sure you know this. It is difficult to believe that we have managed to develop such a friendship without seeing each other in over a year, and after only meeting a couple of times in person. But even harder to believe is the fact there aren't more friendships between Israelis and Palestinians. We live so close to each other. We are so similar.

I believe that, with time, there will be more and more relationships like ours. And it will not be restricted to random friendships – the walls will fall down, and trust will start building up, and eventually, we will not only be neighbouring peoples but also friendly peoples. What is the alternative?

See you next Saturday!

Love,
Daniela

★   ★   ★

August 23rd, 2009
Ramallah

Daniela,

I don't know what to tell you. The Qalandiya check-point is very crowded. There is one passage for those who come to Ramallah, and another for those who leave – just like at a border between two countries.

Everyone goes through a security check and all bags and parcels are x-rayed, like at an airport. The only difference is that this all happens outside, and everyone is exposed to the elements, sun, rain or wind.

Sometimes it doesn't take very long to cross, and other times it can take hours. It depends on the situation on the day and the mood of the soldiers on duty. And also on their personalities and their level of humanity . . . but let's try.

I will try to cross Qalandiya, and meet you on the other side, because this is as far as I can go. If I can cross, then you will not have to go through the unpleasant experience of crossing the check-point. But this doesn't mean that I can then go into Israel – for that I would need a special permit and, frankly, I don't want to beg for an Israeli permit.

Do you know, just the thought of asking for a permit to enter Israel makes me feel sick. After all, this is the place where my grandparents lived just over sixty years ago. And now I have to ask those who chased them away for a permit to step onto that very piece of land? I would really rather not.

So, I will meet you just on the other side of the check-point, if I can make it across. And if they don't let me cross, then perhaps you can try. This might even be better, because if you can get past the check-point, you'll be able to come back home with me. For you, crossing Qalandiya would be the end of the trouble. For me, even if I can cross it, it would be just the beginning. After Qalandiya there are several other road-blocks and check-points before you can enter Israel.

Of course, I too will have my mobile phone on me, so we can coordinate.

And if we fail to cross Qalandiya, at least we'll be able to wave to each other from afar. And the children will be able to see each other from either side. It may be difficult for them, but what can we do? This is our reality.

See you on Saturday,
Shireen

Daniela Norris and Shireen Anabtawi

* The correspondence between Shireen and Daniela started a few months before the war in Gaza at the end of 2008. They both know that no one side is completely right or completely wrong, and that both hold some blame. They refused to let these events spoil their friendship, and despite the pain and the sympathy they both felt for their own people and their suffering, they decided not to damage their friendship by exchanging accusations, which could not change the harsh reality on the ground. They kept in touch during the long weeks of the Gaza war, and despite the difficult feelings, have decided not to write at length about these events in their letters to each other.

They both hope that this was the last war between their peoples, a war that will pave the way to peace with the blood and pain of its victims. They hope that it will help show the way to the establishment of two states, which can live side by side in mutual respect.

This book is dedicated to the memory of all the victims of the long and bloody conflict.

ACKNOWLEDGEMENTS

These letters were initially written for us, and us alone. Later, we decided to try and share them with others. We would not have been able to do so without the support and encouragement of those who believed in the importance of our exchange and helped turn it into a book. Rachel Yona-Michael, Lucy Abrahams and the beloved Jean Currie who did not live to see the publication of this book – we couldn't have done it without you. Our Geneva-based mentors Dr. Zeki Ergas, Ambassador Ibrahim Khraishi and the very inspiring Susan Tiberghien– many thanks for your support. To our publisher Rosie Whitehouse, publicist Jennifer Sandford and last – but not least – our wonderful editor at Reportage Press, Laura Keeling – a heartfelt thank you.

To our husbands and children, who have put up with our distracted minds and often long absences while working on this book – we love you and appreciate your understanding and encouragement.

To our parents, who have taught us to respect 'the other' – even if we believe they are different, even if we believe they are wrong. We will do our utmost to transmit the same message to our children.

And, to our relatives and friends on both sides of the conflict: may we all turn into one big family one day, living and celebrating life together in one of the world's most beautiful and magical regions.

DONATION

CHILDREN OF PEACE

Daniela and Shireen have chosen to donate five percent of the profits from *Crossing Qalandiya: Exchanges Across the Israeli–Palestinian Divide* to Children of Peace.

Children of Peace was established to offer a fresh, non-partisan approach to conflict resolution in the Middle East. It is a UK based, multi faith and moderate charity that works with both Israeli and Palestinian children to build positive relationships for a future generation, whose communities might live and work in peace, side-by-side.

As mothers of young children, Daniela and Shireen are especially aware of the importance of nurturing tolerance and understanding in the new generation.

For more information or to make a donation to Children of Peace, please visit www.childrenofpeace.org.uk.

REPORTAGE PRESS

REPORTAGE PRESS is a new publishing house specialising in books on foreign affairs or set in foreign countries; nonfiction, fiction, essays, travel books, or just books written from a stranger's point of view. Good books like this are now hard to come by – largely because British publishers have become frightened of publishing books that will not guarantee massive sales.

At REPORTAGE PRESS we are not averse to taking risks in order to bring our readers the books they want to read. A percentage of the profits from each of our books goes to a relevant charity chosen by the author.

Our DESPATCHES series brings classic pieces of journalism from the past back into print.

You can buy further copies of *Crossing Qalandiya: Exchanges Across the Israeli/Palestinian Divide* directly from our website, www.reportagepress.com, where you can also find out more about our authors and upcoming titles.

REPORTAGE PRESS

ALSO FROM REPORTAGE PRESS

Something is Going to Fall Like Rain
By Ros Wynne-Jones

'An authentic, well-written and deeply-felt portrait of the tragedy that is South Sudan' – John Le Carré

'A book of meat and emotion, blood and fire – it is a story of our time. And a masterpiece' – Tony Parsons

In Adek, a tiny village in the sprawling desert of Southern Sudan, a community lives on a knife-edge of starvation and war, at the mercy of the bombs that fall from the sky like rain. When three western aidworkers are stranded here – a place where poets carry Kalashnikovs and rebel commanders wear pink dressing gowns – their presence brings hope and danger in equal measure. An ominous ode to Africa's violent beauty, Something is Going to Fall Like Rain is also a life-affirming reminder that love and happiness can co-exist with famine and conflict.

Part of the proceeds from Something is Going to Fall Like Rain go to Oxfam.

Paperback £12.99

ALSO FROM REPORTAGE PRESS

Genocide: My Stolen Rwanda
By Révérien Rurangwa

'The eyes of your assassin. They stay in your mind's eye until death'

Rwanda, April 1994. For thirteen days Révérien Rurangwa hid in silence with his family in a hut on the hillside in Mugina. Eventually they were hunted down by their Hutu neighbours and in minutes forty-three members of his family were massacred before his eyes.

Révérien was the only one to escape, missing a hand and an eye. He was just fifteen years old. In this extraordinary memoir he reflects upon his experience as a survivor uprooted in exile, and attempts to confront the enigmatic power of evil which has steered the course of his life.

Part of the proceeds from *Genocide: My Stolen Rwanda* go to Ibuka – Memory and Justice.

Paperback £8.99

ALSO FROM REPORTAGE PRESS

To the End of Hell
One Woman's Struggle to Survive Cambodia's Khmer Rouge
By Denise Affonço

'The sober and moving retelling of a nightmare survived' – the Economist

In one of the most harrowing memoirs of persecution ever written, Denise Affonço recounts how her comfortable life was torn apart when the Khmer Rouge seized power in Cambodia in April 1975. A French citizen, she was offered the choice of fleeing the country with her children or staying by her husband's side. Chinese and a convinced communist, he believed that the Khmer Rouge would bring an end to five years of civil war. She decided the family should stay together. But peace did not return and along with millions of their fellow citizens they were deported to the countryside to a living hell where they endured almost four years of hard labour, famine, sickness and death.

Part of the proceeds from *To the End of Hell* go to the The Documentation Center of Cambodia, where a scholarship has been set up in the name of Denise Affonço's nine year old daughter Jeannie, who starved to death in 1976 under the Khmer Rouge regime.

Paperback £8.99